WAY TO THE BETTER

THE SPENNYMOOR SETTLEMENT

D1465391

by Robert McManners and Gillian Wales

By the same authors:-

Tom McGuinness - The art of an underground miner
Memories of Witton Park
Shafts of Light - Mining art in the Great Northern Coalfield
McGuinness - Interpreting the art of Tom McGuinness

Published by Gemini Productions

ISBN 978-0-9532217-6-9

Designed and Printed by **hpm**group. 0191 3006941

Dedicated to sisters Ivy Foster and Nancy Gray
who almost trod the Everyman boards.

acknowledgements

The main purpose of this book is to make a historical record of the creation and early years of the Spennymoor Settlement, in particular up to 1954 when it was supported and funded by The Pilgrim Trust and other organisations. We are grateful for the vast array of archive material which has been made available to us and which has allowed us to make a detailed, accurate and extensive account of the Settlement's crucial early years – years in which the validity of this bold, far-reaching sociological experiment was proven.

After funding ceased and the Settlement became a voluntarily funded organisation, the legacy of Bill Farrell was to continue via a group of committed individuals who recognised the Settlement's value as a vital community resource. In the second part of the book we outline some of the multifarious activities from 1954 to the present day and attempt to identify key personnel and Settlement highlights during those years but acknowledge that it is not possible to record every individual contribution and activity. We are none the less grateful and would like to thank and pay tribute to those members of the Spennymoor Settlement – too numerous to mention by name - who have contributed so generously to the research and production of this book, in particular those who responded to requests for information - written, oral and pictorial - to ensure its accuracy.

Particular thanks to Arnold Hadwin and thanks for use of images to Bob Abley, Rene Chaplin and Norman Cornish. Finally, sincere thanks to our proof readers, Glynn Wales, Stefa McManners and Lynne Goodes for their patient and meticulous reading of the text.

Robert McManners and Gillian Wales
October 2008

foreword

The Spennymoor Settlement ("the Pitman's Academy") shaped innumerable lives, mine included, so it is a great privilege to be associated with this history of a remarkable, ahead-of–its-time venture. We owe the compilers of this volume the greatest respect. It is an obvious labour of love, full of hard-come-by information and insights.

The Settlement means many things to many different people from all walks of life. It is the embodiment of the old adage: "Life is a nettle; touch it and it stingeth, grasp it firmly and it stingeth not."

I have never ceased to be amazed at my good fortune to have been born before the Settlement came to Spennymoor which enabled me, at about the age of four, to be a member of its innovative pre-school play group and thereafter to be involved in most of the activities that broadened horizons and gave access to the world of ideas, the Arts and personal responsibility and commitment.

It would have been easy for the Settlement to have been pretentious and elitist, but it was never that. It was always against ignorance, intolerance and bigotry; always for learning, understanding and compassion. Idealism and pragmatism walked hand in hand; there was intelligent compromise without betrayal of principle. Every member had something distinctive to offer, had talents that had to be nurtured and harnessed, had something exciting to learn. The going was sometimes hard and demanding but there was a lot of fun.

My memories take in a range of subjects from scouting and drama, film and music groups to W.E.A. classes, struggles against injustice and what Ruskin labelled as "the impotent, churl mind." What comes to mind is awakening on a dew-drenched Scout campsite during wartime, everything proclaiming that it was good to be alive and be at one with Nature. And, from a later date at the Everyman Theatre, being impressed indelibly with the Cassius truism: "It is not in our stars, but in ourselves that we are underlings." The Settlement gave an impoverished community the will and the means to fight back against the failings of the State, with assurance and dignity.

I cannot imagine what my life would have been like without the influence of the Settlement; and I think most other members would say the same. Values, crying out to be passed on, were instilled making life meaningful and challenging. Who could ask for more?

The Settlement sought to empower Everyman to have a hand in determining his or her destiny. It stressed the need for commitment in the old fashioned sense, based on reason, compassion, effort and, most of all, a set of values, not to be imposed upon others, but to be urged upon them by persuasion, argument and personal example. That is sometimes an arduous path to tread but it was the Settlement's way.

I hope this book is read not only in County Durham but in every community that aspires to self improvement and the sharing of fellowship and understanding.

Arnold Hadwin

contents

chapter one - The inception of the settlement movement   page 1

chapter two - Education for all   page 9

chapter three - The Spennymoor Settlement: the early days   page 15

chapter four - The Sketching Club   page 23

chapter five - The Members' Association   page 27

chapter six - The Everyman Players   page 33

chapter seven - The Pitman's Academy   page 43

chapter eight - A slice of life   page 53

chapter nine - Miner and child   page 61

chapter ten - Learning and literature   page 71

chapter eleven - Means Test to majesty   page 77

chapter twelve - The last act   page 83

chapter thirteen - Exit – stage right   page 87

chapter fourteen - The final curtain   page 91

chapter fifteen - The play must go on   page 95

chapter sixteen - The curtain rises   page 101

chapter seventeen - Encore   page 107

postscript   page 115

appendices

Appendix 1: Productions by Settlement Players   page 117

Appendix 2: "… way to the better…" being some account
of the Founding, Achievements and Aims
of the Spennymoor Settlement   page 122

Appendix 3: Curtain Calls   page 127

bibliography   page 139

All quotes in the text are attributable to Bill Farrell unless otherwise stated.

authors' introduction

Way to the Better

The Spennymoor Settlement is a sociological phenomenon.

From its inception on 1st April 1931 to its rebirth in 2008 the Settlement has been a fountain of cultural opportunity, social welfare, economic survival and educational inspiration. The impact was to radiate from Spennymoor to the communities of South West Durham and far beyond. Out of the visionary aspiration of the Warden Bill Farrell was to flow a torrent of cultural enlightenment which would have far-reaching effects on the future of both individuals and the community at large.

This book presents an opportunity to record the history, contextualise the background and explore the legacy of the Spennymoor Settlement. We trace the antecedent, disparate institutions for adult education that existed in the latter part of the nineteenth century resulting in the inception of the Settlement Movement. The social dichotomy that was extant in Victorian England – in which the material wealth of the newly industrialised society contrasted starkly with the abject poverty of an exploited substratum of the lower orders – had spawned this raft of religious and philanthropic attempts at rescue.

It is of the stuff of fantasy that a small theatre in a small Durham town could host Old Vic productions, exhibit work by artists of international repute and help convince a German Countess, Elisabeth von der Schulenberg, whose brother was involved in the celebrated Stauffenberg attempt to assassinate Hitler, to give up her life of ease for that of a working nun!

The Spennymoor Settlement proffered enlightenment – an enlightenment which was to be the catalyst for artists of the calibre of Norman Cornish and Tom McGuinness and a writer as talented as Sid Chaplin to realise their full potential - their own 'way to the better'.

Robert McManners and Gillian Wales

chapter one

The inception of the settlement movement

Caravan City, Spennymoor, 1935 (Photo courtesy of Durham University Library)

"It was the best of times; it was the worst of times."
Charles Dickens

It is difficult for us to imagine the deprivation and the abject squalor that was the everyday life of many of the disadvantaged in the Victorian era. The rapid industrialisation of England – the first country to undergo such a revolution – brought sweeping changes which no one in the nation could avoid or ignore. The social and demographic upheaval of such sudden change had seen no precedent. The infrastructure at the time of this rapid urbanisation was totally inadequate and the established social order, based on rural feudalism, was overturned. The new hierarchy was to be constituted from the industrial barons who became the power base in society. It was from this context of massive social upheaval that the Settlement Movement evolved.

The Spennymoor Settlement

Workers had to live within walking distance of their employment and consequently the working classes lived cheek by jowl with their places of work – often clamorous, foul, filthy factories constantly wallowing in the pall of their own polluting smoke. This was not an environment where those with financial independence would choose to live. In the large conurbations this produced a distinct division, dictated by the prevailing wind, between the areas where working classes and middle classes dwelt– as in London and indeed Newcastle - an East End for the workers and a West End for the wealthy. The communities rarely mixed and had little or no understanding of each others' lives.

Samuel & Henrietta Barnett

The precipitant migration of rural workers to the industrial urban centres created a crisis in housing, often exacerbated by the magnates of industry who provided very poor accommodation in tied houses or substandard lodgings which led to the creation of the slum districts of many of the large cities so graphically portrayed in the novels of social observers like Charles Dickens – conditions not unlike those found in the 'distressed areas' of 1930s Britain. But this was reality not the stuff of fiction. Exploitation of the employees was rife and even those in regular work often found themselves at the level of subsistence – education was therefore a relative luxury and was available to a fortunate few. There was no social support, very little regulation of working conditions or remuneration, scant access to medical care and formal education, if provided at all, ended at the age of eleven. There was to be an increasing awareness of these issues amongst many concerned groups and organisations especially religious groups like the Quakers, individual philanthropists and educational establishments such as the universities.

The first of the Mechanics Institutes, for example, had been founded in Glasgow in 1823. These were educational establishments formed to provide adult education, particularly in technical subjects, to working men. They were often funded by local industrialists and philanthropists, such as Robert Stephenson, James Nasmyth and Joseph Whitworth, on the grounds that they, the employers, by providing the workers with an alternative to gambling and drinking, would ultimately benefit from having more knowledgeable and skilled employees.

Although the first residential Settlement - Toynbee Hall, a University Settlement - was not established until 1884, a catalyst had effectively appeared in the guise of Samuel Augustus Barnett as early as 1873. That year Barnett was inducted as curate to the living of Saint Jude in

London's East End, at his own request. It was a parish described by the then Bishop of London as "the worst parish in my diocese, inhabited mainly by a criminal population and one which has, I fear, been much corrupted by doles." Barnett and his wife, Henrietta, found extreme poverty and hardship in their new parish, much worse than the Bishop had described. The people were poor, for the most part unemployed, even in times of prosperity, feckless, depraved and criminal. Living conditions were the worst of any to be found in East London – overcrowding in old and unsanitary houses and tenements, with all the attendant evils of disease, crime, high infant mortality and an even higher birth rate. Materially, the people of the neighbourhood were poverty stricken – but spiritually, intellectually and culturally their poverty was even greater. Lord Beveridge in his autobiography, 'Power and Influence', commented, "Barnett conceived the idea that one of the things wrong with London was its physical separation into cities of the poor and cities of the well-to-do, an East End and a West End. This meant that the former lacked men of leisure and education for their necessary common activities; it meant that the latter were ignorant of the nature and consequences of poverty." Some men of wealth and intellect such as Edward Dennison and J. R. Green who were practising Christian Socialists had already begun to 'settle' in Stepney in the East End. Indeed, in 1868, having been invited to the home of social reformer and critic John Ruskin to discuss ways of helping the poor, they proposed to Ruskin the idea of a 'settlement'. The discussions did not produce their hoped-for result but other educated men followed their example and continued to 'settle' in the East End.

Canon Barnett began to directly involve himself in the introduction of 'settlers' into the East End. He had taken the opportunity while visiting Oxford University in 1875 to meet with Arnold Toynbee, [1852-1883], a prominent socialist undergraduate, and with his circle of friends whom Barnett invited to his Whitechapel parish during their vacations. Many took up Barnett's invitation to help with the various clubs, assist at parties and to visit on behalf of the Charity Organisation Society. Indeed, Toynbee himself became a frequent visitor to this future settlement in embryo. The massive wave of social conscience which was to follow the publication in October 1883 of the pamphlet 'The Bitter Cry of Outcast London: an inquiry into the conditions of the abject poor' and a newspaper campaign that focused attention on the problem of the East End of London particularly, was the motive force that helped action the movement.

John Ruskin

When Barnett was asked to address a group of undergraduates in Oxford in 1883 it was the ideal opportunity to propose the founding of a Settlement, a more systemised form of what was already

3

William Beveridge

happening in his parish of Saint Jude. In the paper he presented, 'Settlements of university men in great towns', he stated, "A Settlement is simply a means by which men or women may share themselves with their neighbours; a club-house in an industrial district, where the condition of membership is the performance of a citizen's duty; a house among the poor where residents may make friends with the poor. ...The revelation of recent pamphlets have fallen on ears prepared to hear." Educated opinion had become conscious for the first time on a national scale that something was wrong with the distribution of wealth in England. Barnett pointed out in his paper, "The fact that the wealth of England means only wealth in England and that the mass of the people live without knowledge, without hope, and often without health has come home to open minds and consciences." As a result of Barnett's paper an informal meeting took place at Balliol on 3rd December 1883 at which it was resolved to found a University Settlement in East London. It was to be called Toynbee Hall in memory of Arnold Toynbee who had recently died.

A council was formed of prominent university men and Barnett was invited to become Warden. "Barnett contrived the foundation of a Settlement where men of University type – civil servants, barristers, doctors and so on – while pursuing their avocations, could live together and become citizens of the East End rather than the West End," stated Lord Beveridge who himself became sub warden at Toynbee Hall in 1903. "Sentimental philanthropy," snorted his father when the new graduate announced he was opting for settlement work rather than the law or academia as his chosen career. Beveridge's time there and his contact with the unemployed gained him valuable experience, however, which inspired him to formulate his future development of the Welfare State.

J. A. R. Pimlott, the historian of Toynbee Hall, wrote, "The Settlement Movement arose out of these three fundamental needs: the need for scientific research, the need for a wider life through education, and the need for leadership. For it was only if men of a wider education than themselves lived among the population whom it was desired to help that any of these fundamental requirements could be adequately satisfied." Barnett's proposed solution was to approach the resources of the university to attack the root cause rather than look for a philanthropic palliation as Christian Johnson writes in his book on the Settlement movement 'Strength in Community', "...[Barnett's] reason for turning to the universities for help in meeting the larger issues of poverty was because ... their resources of human power and enjoyment represented what he wanted for everybody ... he proposed the establishment of a University Settlement in his parish so that privileged students and disadvantaged local residents could live as neighbours and improve local conditions together."

Samuel Barnett, like Beatrice and Sidney Webb and the Fabians - who were later to found the London School of Economics - saw the immense possibilities of local government and believed that settlements could provide some civic leadership. This was to be achieved through the education and stimulation of electors and the participation of the residents with local people in local government. This concern for 'practical socialism' led to considerable activity. Unlike the later Spennymoor Settlement, Toynbee Hall's programme was primarily cultural, academic and educational, delivered in a social context and included training of teachers and social workers, assistance to Jewish immigrants and to the formation of literary and dramatic societies. Training in practical skills was not offered. The

Arnold Toynbee

Toynbee Hall (Photo courtesy of Toynbee Hall)

ethos of the University Settlement at Toynbee Hall was that "…university men might get to know workmen and their problems through contact and discussion and through teaching, research, public service and sociability, contribute something in return …Toynbee Hall was oriented, not to the parish or district, but toward the institutional structure of the nation …The residents came 'to learn as much as to teach, to receive as much as to give.' They lived in the neighbourhood in order to know as much as possible about it, as a spring board bringing about changes in the mores and the institutional structure of the nation." Whilst these principles may appear impractical and theoretical in today's society, they are undoubtedly based on lasting sound ethical and religious tenets and their validity can be confirmed by the growth and longevity of the Settlement Movement which resulted in the opening of dozens of institutions – many of which survive to this day.

Sidney & Beatrice Webb

Toynbee Hall attracted a number of very able and committed settlers, many of whom became deeply involved with social inquiry and the development of thinking and policy about the alleviation of poverty. It gained a reputation as a training ground for bright, young, reform-minded civil servants. The residents' list reads like a roll call of key figures in the making of the welfare state: William Beveridge, R.H. Tawney, Clement Atlee and Kenneth Lindsay all spent time there. Albert Mansfield, a former student of Toynbee Hall, established the Workers' Education Association in 1903 – the Settlement provided the Association with an office and organised its library to act as a central library for the W.E.A. Public libraries, the Whitechapel Art Gallery and children's homes were some of the original projects that grew out of Toynbee Hall and advice was often available on legal problems and welfare rights; this was to lead directly to the formation of the Citizens' Advice Bureau network.

Amongst Toynbee Hall's visitors and residents were many from abroad. The Movement's ideals and principles were quickly exported to other industrialised countries including the United States, France, Russia, Germany and Japan – indeed in the United States there were over 400 such establishments by 1910. By the early twentieth century there were over forty established settlements in Great Britain, with the majority being located in London. London was then the world's largest city but the same social problems associated with rapid industrialisation and urbanisation that afflicted the capital were also endemic in provincial cities where heavy industries dominated. New industrial processes spawned completely new industries and employment opportunities but the rapid changes in technology meant many of these industries were short-lived with the consequent social deprivation that contributed to the rise of the Settlement Movement. Initially the individual settlements were autonomous organisations adhering to a common ethos but the mushroom growth of the early years of the twentieth century saw the formation of associations whose prime aim was to influence the thinking of local and national government in the context of social welfare.

In the United Kingdom the Federation of Residential Settlements was formed in 1920, this was later to be renamed the British Association of Residential Settlements and is known today as the British Association of Settlements and Social Action Centres – BASSAC. The same year saw the formation of the Educational Settlements Association which, as its name implies, was an affiliation of settlements primarily concerned with adult education rather than the provision of a residential facility. The influence of the educational settlements was to become increasingly important, particularly in the period between the World Wars - witness the establishment of the Spennymoor Settlement in 1931 - and they were the forerunners of the community centres and local authority adult educational centres of today.

The Quaker adult schools were the progenitors of the educational settlements. The movement started in the North of England with the financial support of philanthropic benefactors such as Joseph Rowntree, the Quaker chocolate and confectionery manufacturer from York. The Rowntree family were respected for their involvement in adult education from the very early years of the twentieth century. In 1903 the family had sponsored the establishment of the Woodbrooke Settlement in Birmingham, a non-residential college for Quakers and others, at the instigation of the visionary John Wilhelm Rowntree, and with a curriculum based on religious values. In 1904 the Joseph Rowntree Charitable Trust was established and eventually became the source of finance for the educational settlements. The following year the influential John Rowntree died and his fellow Quakers inaugurated the Yorkshire Friends Service Committee (originally the Yorkshire 1905 Committee) which was established specifically to further education and promote social service within the Quaker community in Yorkshire. Initially the organisation had no physical base and it was soon realised that, for the initiative to thrive, permanent premises were needed.

As a result, the Swarthmore Settlement was established in Leeds in 1909 and in the same year the Saint Mary's Settlement opened in York. Both of these establishments survived because of the continuing guidance of the Rowntree family. The curriculum, initially centred on Christian teaching, expanded to include history, economics, science, literature and notably music. Whilst this broadening of the curriculum widened the educational scope of these two establishments, the claim to be the first true educational settlement comes from the North West, where founder Horace Fleming felt that the greater breadth of educational opportunity provided at the Beechcroft Settlement in Birkenhead made it "a more genuine community centre of adult education."

In the next few years many more educational settlements were founded throughout the length of the country - from Gateshead to Plymouth - and, by 1935, the Educational Settlements Association, ESA, had thirty two members. Such was its authority that, in 1924, it was designated one of the 'Responsible Bodies' which entitled it to statutory financial support for the provision of adult education.

The consequence of the General Strike of 1926 and the associated eighteen month long Miners' Strike was mass unemployment and poverty, particularly in the coalfield areas where many collieries had closed as a result of the industrial action. The worst hit areas included South Wales and South West Durham. This gave a new dimension to the aims of the educational settlements. In 1927 an educational settlement was established at Trealaw in the Rhondda Valley, one of nine created between 1927 and 1937 in the Welsh valleys - the Maes-yr-Haf Settlement. Although based on educational principles, this was augmented by a strong emphasis on mutual aid and social action and the settlement workers became involved with the very survival of their members and found themselves providing a soup kitchen alongside classes in subsistence to improve the long-term welfare and prospects of the unemployed. This resulted in the pioneering formation of clubs for unemployed men in which practical skills such as joinery and cobbling were taught. Physical fitness through exercise was seen as an important aspect of self-esteem and personal survival, as was an opportunity to become involved in all aspects of music and drama. We can see in this model the forerunner of the Spennymoor Settlement.

Settlements in the government-designated 'special areas' were able to attract additional funding both from grant-making trusts such as the Pilgrim Trust – for example the Spennymoor Settlement – and, from 1934 onwards, from the Special Areas Commissioners who were government appointees responsible for distributing grants to these distressed areas. The fundamental educational settlement ethos was to continue but the religious dimension was to wane because of the different needs of the clientele and the changing times and values.

chapter two

Education for all

Bill Farrell

"The Settlement is your university.
Its facilities are almost free to you.
It may offer you the one chance of your life.
What will you do about it?"

Spennymoor is an industrial town in the south west of County Durham. A product of the Industrial Revolution, it owes its existence to the mineral deposits in the locality. Coal had been mined in the area for centuries, mainly to the west of Spennymoor, where it was readily accessible in the 'exposed coalfield'. Spennymoor itself came into existence with the sinking of the Whitworth pit in 1839 which resulted in rough housing being built for the workers on the moorland site. In 1853 the Weardale Iron and Coal Company opened the Tudhoe Iron Works. At its peak it was the largest iron mill in Europe and this led to a mushroom development of the town. The Works accounted for the most prosperous period of the town's history, providing employment for thousands of men and hence livelihood for thousands of families in the locality. Housing needs were met by the hasty construction of dreary terraces in ribbon development along the main roads.

The opening of new collieries at nearby Page Bank and Tudhoe resulted in the influx of many immigrant workers from the Midlands, Wales and Lancashire. In this period, the 1860s and 1870s, the population of the town reached over 18,000. To quote from Keith Armstrong's 'Homespun', "…the town was ringed with collieries, black furnaces and coke ovens and the new prosperity showed itself in the building of better houses and the opening of the Co-operative Stores. The comparative isolation of its moorland situation ended too with the opening of the branch railway from the main line at Ferryhill in 1876." This prosperity, however, was not to last. The 1880s and 1890s were dogged by the beginnings of an economic decline, a disastrous explosion at Tudhoe Colliery and a strike that paralysed the area."

The 20th century was to herald the start of an even longer, more profound, period of depression and social distress for the town, beginning with the abrupt closure of the Tudhoe Iron Works in 1901. At the same time the reduced demand for coking coal resulted in the closure of many coal mines and short-time working in others. This trend was exacerbated by the General Strike of 1926

The demolition of Tudhoe Iron Works

and Spennymoor became one of the most disadvantaged towns in the South West Durham 'distressed area' where 'long unemployment' was endemic. 'Long unemployment' was defined as unemployment for more than one year. In the 1931 census the population for the Spennymoor Urban District was 28,911 - 10,974 were insured workers. Of these 3,367 were unemployed representing almost one third of the workforce. Significantly 70% of the workless were 'long unemployed'. The unemployed man's life was not a life of leisure but a one of apathy and poverty. "Time," one of the 'long unemployed' said, "is my worst enemy now … We go for walks and dig in our gardens. But mostly we sit about."

There was a prevailing air of pessimism that Spennymoor had no future, the coal industry would not revive and therefore there would be no demand for miners and that they and their families should relocate. This position was reinforced in a

Tisa Hess - Sketch of unemployed men, Spennymoor, 1937

series of articles in The Times of March 1934 entitled 'Places without a future'. The correspondent advocated that the area should revert to agriculture. In 1936 the third report of the Commissioner for Special Areas stated, "Some of the village communities in South West Durham must face the fact that they have no industrial future and that their district must revert to the agricultural life which prevailed up till a century ago." These ideas were not questioned and appeared to have been generally accepted. It was this atmosphere of despair, desperation and indeed futility that William George Farrell found himself investigating on behalf of the Pilgrim Trust in 1930.

The Pilgrim Trust was founded in 1930 by Edward Stephen Harkness, an American philanthropist, whose ancestors had emigrated to America from Dumfries, Scotland in 1761. A New Yorker, Edward had inherited his wealth from his father who was assistant to oil tycoon John D. Rockfeller. Massive investment in the American railroad system had enhanced the Harkness fortune. Edward and his wife were childless and decided upon 'systematic philanthropy' to distribute this vast wealth. The majority of the gifts were made to American causes. In the late 1920s, however, Edward was moved by the increasing number of appeals for financial help that reached him from Britain but, lacking the background knowledge to discriminate between deserving and worthless appeals, Edward decided to endow £2 million to a selected Board of British Trustees to administer the fund wisely. The first Chairman of the Trust was Stanley Baldwin because Edward Harkness regarded Baldwin as the most respected man in English public life. Harkness took no part in the management of the Trust nor did he wish his name to be associated with it. At his wife's suggestion it was called the Pilgrim Trust to signify its link with the land of the Pilgrim Fathers and its dedication to an adventurous ideal. Until the outbreak of the Second World

War the Trustees expended their income equally between the preservation of National Heritage and schemes for the welfare of the unemployed.

Bill Farrell was born on 10th March 1895 in Liverpool. Educated at a church school, his further formal academic education was interrupted by voluntary active service in France and Belgium during the First World War in which he served in the infantry as a Battalion Messing Corporal. He went on to study accountancy and office routines for seven years with a Liverpool shipping company, during which time his social awareness developed, resulting in personal involvement in voluntary social service, together with a passionate interest in the performing and visual arts. In 1927 Bill Farrell left the world of commerce for a full time career in the theatre, initially joining Terence Gray's theatrical company at the Festival Theatre, Cambridge, before going on to work in London theatre. Whilst working in the capital he stayed at Toynbee Hall, the university's settlement in Whitechapel, East London, where he undertook voluntary social work and teaching whilst 'resting' between engagements.

The founder of Toynbee Hall, Canon Samuel Augustus Barnett, had envisaged a centre in which "university men could live side by side with their neighbours in the district, making friends with them, entering with them into duties of citizens; organising together educational classes, lectures, debates, concerts, clubs and parties." It was to be a place where "men and women of every creed, party, race and faith could come together for discussion and to learn to understand one another. It was not to be, in any sense, a group of those who had giving to those who had not. It was to be a co-operative effort in which all who came …would give and receive friendship,

Norman Cornish - Colliery Back Street, Mixed Media

knowledge, and understanding." These aims crystallised Bill Farrell's own personal philosophy.

In the summer of 1930 Bill Farrell toured the provinces " …to study the conditions of work of theatrical touring companies and to determine the reasons for professional depression." Thus when, in the winter of 1930, the Pilgrim Trust made available a large grant to enable a survey of conditions in the Durham Coalfield to be undertaken with a view to establishing a settlement along the lines of Toynbee Hall in the area of perceived greatest need, Bill Farrell was selected as the obvious person to undertake the survey.

In his first hand-written report to Toynbee Hall on 28th April 1931, Bill Farrell saw the unemployed miner as drifting aimlessly and felt the miner "… needed to be encouraged and helped to think of other things and other spheres of possible work besides the defunct or moribund mine."

Sir Wyndham Deedes (Photo courtesy of The Daily Telegraph)

He focused on Spennymoor, finding that "…the present industrial situation is grave in the extreme …of the insured population thirty five percent, chiefly miners, are unemployed and have been for some time. They have lost 'skill hunger'. They have few hobbies and little appetite for games, generally inert – perhaps because there is little to do and nowhere to go – not even a public library with a newspaper. They lounge in the main street or throng doorways of public houses and billiard saloons. There is real reason to dread the consequences of the present idle and aimless lives of so large a population." Bill Farrell was expressing his personal concern for the well-being of the individual in a disadvantaged society but was also perhaps warning of his fears for social stability and national integrity if civil unrest was to erupt from these disillusioned people.

This view was formally reinforced by Sir Wyndham Deedes of the National Council of Social Service when he expressed the same concern from a different perspective. He perceived the political and social dangers for a society that resisted the education and empowerment of such a group. He argued against the notion that unemployment benefit and other forms of State support were all that was necessary. "Did they realise that men were living in abject poverty, deprived not merely of physical things but of all those opportunities and means whereby man could fulfil his destiny? That the problem of unemployment could never be solved by ourselves alone or by any one section of society. It could only be solved when those who were themselves suffering and alone knew what unemployment really meant joined with those who were not."

"Far too many people look upon men as workers and not as men. People have only begun to see they are not only workers, and amongst those out of their ordinary occupation in circumstances beyond their control are artists and painters, and they have every conceivable gift donated by

God. They have never previously had the opportunity to express themselves. They have only been 'hewers of wood and drawers of water'. There was not common effort or that oneness which was so characteristic of movement abroad." Indeed Sir Wyndham Deedes' speech was reassuring to those in society at this time who appeared to be fearful of the perceived danger of educating the unemployed – those who likened the unemployed miners to the revolutionaries of Russia, France and Italy and who warned of the dangers of empowerment through education, with an unstated agenda of preserving the social and possibly political status quo.

chapter three

The Spennymoor Settlement: the early days

The Spennymoor Settlement, King Street, Spennymoor

The Settlement finally opened at the behest of two unemployed miners who, aware of the publicity, knocked on the door and requested entry. The official opening date is recorded as 1st April 1931.

As a result of Bill Farrell's investigation into and report on the needs of Spennymoor, he was charged with the task of forming a settlement in the town. Just as Sir Wyndham Deedes had found fears in the minds of employed members of society about alerting the unemployed to their own potential – a fear spawned from such mass demonstration of the power of disillusionment as the Jarrow March – Bill Farrell found the repressed unemployed equally as wary. He felt it necessary to live in Spennymoor for some time to enable himself to become accepted by the local unemployed population - a population that had never previously experienced altruism and regarded the incomer with a healthy scepticism - before the settlement could be truly inaugurated. This lack of trust on both sides of the employment divide determined Bill Farrell to avoid any such separation in the Spennymoor Settlement and everyone, whether employed or not, from whatever walk of life and from whatever district, would be welcomed to the settlement. This avoidance of the employment distinction was an integral aspect of the national settlement ethic.

We learn about Bill Farrell's personal philosophy from his curriculum vitae of the late 1930s. He believed "...the individual has rights which are inviolable, and therefore holds allegiance to no political party and to no religious denomination. Will not subject to authoritarianism of church or state. Believes that the only hope for a very distressed world is a return to the Arts of Peace, the steady cultivation of international thinking, immediate action along the lines of Christ's teaching, shorn of dogmatical accretions, and in the extensive enlightenment of all peoples without reference to nationality, class, creed, colour or party." From these personal beliefs Bill Farrell formulated the official objectives of the Spennymoor Settlement which were "To encourage tolerant neighbourliness and voluntary social service and give its members opportunities for increasing their knowledge, widening their interests and cultivating their creative powers in a friendly atmosphere."

Whilst the sociological and educational objectives are overt in this statement the methodology to achieve those objectives is not stated. Models of delivery similar to that which Bill Farrell was to adopt already existed albeit with different aims. The Arts and Crafts Movement at the turn of the century had drawn together all aspects of creativity – both theoretical and practical - and these concepts had been taken up by educational establishments in Europe, especially the Wiener Werkstatte in Vienna and The Bauhaus School in Germany. Bill Farrell was to translate their

Edward Street, Spennymoor

objectives into practical action. His first priority was appropriate premises. This proved difficult in practice as no large house suitable for conversion was available in Spennymoor and consequently the first building the Settlement was to occupy was a disused shop at 36 – 38 King Street. This accommodation comprised a large room capable of seating fifty, a small back room which could seat thirty, together with an outhouse. The shop area was subsequently used as a Common Room, library, meeting room, rehearsal room and lecture room. The small back room was used as an office, classroom, store room, studio, workroom and music room; the outhouse was used as a cobbler's shop. Bill Farrell and his wife Betty lived in rooms above the Settlement and were available at all times.

The miners came at first for two reasons – curiosity and because there wasn't anything else to do. They were suspicious

Norman Cornish - Sketch of Betty Farrell, Conté, c1936

of everything. The Common Room nearly caused a row because they'd never heard the name and thought it meant a room set aside for common people! Bill Farrell's title of Warden upset some of them too. They confused the word warden with warder. Bill Farrell was no warder, however, and gradually their suspicions faded away. Drastic steps had to be taken to prevent some of the men from turning the Common Room into a bar. Therefore, a small committee was co-opted from among the men themselves, a duty roster was set up and each committee member took it in turns to act as 'host' for one day a week, excluding Sunday. This Working Committee met with the Warden every week to discuss the work of the Settlement. It was firmly impressed upon the minds of these men that the chief aim of the Settlement was an educational one and they were urged to ensure that users of the Common Room also became members of a study or working group. This co-operative spirit was essential if the groups were to remain viable.

"The greatest difficulty lies in convincing men for whom the world seems to have no further use that the unfamiliar and difficult thing at first may be really worthwhile and that it may hold something of interest to them which will enable them to find a new interest in their old, drab, monotonous world. Always at the back of their minds lies the thought that nothing is worthwhile to them, nobody really cares whether they live or die and so what does it matter whether they do anything or not? And in most cases they are more often hungry than not, always anxious how much longer their clothes will last and always wondering whether a mythical 'someone' will set them on."

The Morning Post of 25th January 1934 quoted Bill Farrell, "Spennymoor is the hardest nut to crack in Durham... a squat centipede of a town... Mistrust and misunderstanding between master and workman, the lack of people with leisure and a sense of responsibility in the use of it, made of Spennymoor a place where political bickering and denominational antagonism were the main form of excitement ... we don't so much teach as encourage – draw out... prejudices must be overcome, personal sympathies won. Unemployed miners or ironworkers come singly for advice or merely to talk. They must be listened to slowly, patiently. Haste or preoccupation would touch sensitive spots, begat suspicion ... Everything must be related to daily life and the enlivening of it – there is a debating society – Parliamentary style – the 'mace' is a miner's pick. When the pick is carried in before the Warden (Mr Speaker) the room is instantly quiet and the debate proceeds, with an orderliness that would put Westminster to shame."

Bill Farrell tells us in his document 'Way to the Better' that when they "opened the Settlement doors wide and invited a suspicious, leisureful populace to come in, far too many did. There was not room for them all and so came a decision which coloured the whole of the Settlement's subsequent history. Lack of accommodation and preference also dictated a qualitative rather than a quantitative method." Bill Farrell and his wife were both interested in painting and the theatre and decided to begin by organising educational groups in these subjects and so a Play Reading Group and a Sketching Club were formed. Practical educational classes were commenced with the stocking and opening of a Carpenter's and Cobbler's Shop and with the inception of a Women's Needlework Group – many of the designs for the needlework were created by members of the Sketching Club and were included in Settlement exhibitions, often

Robert Heslop - Page Bank Colliery, Poster Colour, 1950s

Norman Cornish - Berriman's Chip Van, Mixed Media

under the aegis of 'Thrift Work' – making something out of nothing - thus old felt hats were turned into bedroom slippers and dusters were embroidered to form cushion covers.

Other groups – Government Study, Current Affairs and Elementary Psychology were begun. The Spennymoor Settlement also boasted a Male Voice Choir and a Children's Play Centre. These original premises also housed a branch of the County Library, the first lending library in Spennymoor, with the Warden as Honorary Librarian although, to quote Bill Farrell, "The literary taste is for the most part deplorable."

Whether or not the impact of the opening of the Settlement was as Bill Farrell had envisaged is a matter of conjecture. From his reports to Toynbee Hall we can glean that he was very concerned that the steering committee had to be very carefully constituted and briefed to avoid even the smallest mistake. He realised that he had to take along with him local authority representatives and leaders of existing local organisations, such as churches. Bill Farrell's idea was to overcome any resistance to his proposals by co-opting representatives from these organisations onto his executive committee. It would seem that the rather precipitant opening of the Settlement wrong-footed Bill Farrell as his most fervent aim, the need for adequate premises, had, by dint of lack of availability, been denied him. From his own writings, Bill Farrell saw the aim of the Settlement

Movement as that of bringing education to all who wanted it – an open door policy. However, when the doors were opened the facilities were overwhelmed and selection by limiting the subject areas available, subject areas selected by the Warden, was applied. Bill Farrell justifies this selection as expediency but what is not recorded is the fate of the men who turned up to find the Settlement did not meet their expectations or had nothing to offer them. Did they see this as rejection? History does not and never will tell us.

The challenge of organising a programme which would appeal to those without any background in adult education was daunting. The experience of Horace Fleming, the Warden of Beechcroft, the Birkenhead Settlement, was to be mirrored at Spennymoor. "In 1922 there were 10,000 unemployed in Birkenhead and Settlement workers wished to help. Beechcroft being an educational institution was bound to attempt something along educational lines, although our first attempt could not be considered a success. Our error lay in thinking of the rank and file of industrial workers as being on the same intellectual level as the Trades Council members of our weekend lecture schools. We did not allow sufficiently for the depreciation in the power of concentration which invariably accompanies unemployment. The first attempt was a course of university extension lectures … the audience, numbering about 60 to start with, was not equal to sustained attention and the audience declined until there were fewer than 20 at the final lecture." Mr Fleming found that a much simpler course along adult school lines was a great success. Similar difficulties were encountered at Spennymoor.

Children at Play (Photo courtesy of Rene Chaplin)

Many classes or groups were formed and large numbers of students enrolled. The Play Reading Group had 43 members, the Local Government Study Group 78 and the Current Affairs Group 41. As Bill Farrell stated in his first annual report, "The figures given represent the number of persons that enrolled at the beginning; the average number of regular attendances is just about one third of the numbers enrolled." The common factor Bill Farrell agreed was the failure to take into account, "the depreciation of concentration which invariably accompanies unemployment." As a consequence Bill Farrell pragmatically revised his programme and the 'Model Parliament' was transformed into a 'Lecture Society' while the 'Current Affairs Group' became the 'Wireless Listening Group'.

Despite his best efforts Bill Farrell later recognised that his attempts to promote the art of music amongst Settlement members had proved difficult to sustain. Many groups had been started but suffered the same fate as the Instrumental Music Group. In his seventh annual report of 1937/38 Bill Farrell comments on this new group, "…a new venture of the winter term, it has not grown as was hoped, but the few who do attend are keen and with a little encouragement the class may grow into the Settlement Orchestra that is hoped for." Unfortunately this was not to be and no further mention was made of the orchestra in subsequent reports. A male voice choir begun in 1944 also disappears from the pages of the annual reports. The only music group to enjoy any degree of success was the Gramophone Music Group formed in 1947 in which members organised the programme and provided the records themselves, meeting in the theatre after church on a Sunday.

Pitman's Academy Exhibition 1936
(taken from newspaper article, courtesy of The Northern Echo)

Bill Farrell, writing with hindsight in 1942, explains that although Spennymoor Settlement was criticised for not meeting the needs of those who did not wish to take part in some kind of creative activity, they were not forgotten. He saw the Settlement's role as that of a training ground for socially-conscious people who would then go out and join in the fight against the real enemies of society elsewhere – his 'shock brigade'. Several young men and women 'graduated' from the Settlement, winning scholarships to attend Workers' Colleges. Neither, Bill Farrell argues, had the Settlement forgotten all those other disadvantaged people living in different parts of the coalfield, for he toured the county and helped organise more than thirty Social Service Centres which he imbued with some of the Settlement's ideals.

Whilst the main thrust of the education at the Settlement was of an intellectual nature the training needs of living at a subsistence level were not ignored. The practical implication of an unemployed man being able to repair his family's shoes or mend a window frame were not lost on Bill Farrell, hence the importance of the Cobbler's and the Joiner's Shops to the work of the Settlement. The women's group for needlework and crafts had its obvious practical benefits but also produced embroidery of the highest prize winning standard. Bill Farrell also stimulated demand for all these skills within the Settlement programme with the formation of the Theatre Group, later to become the Everyman Players. He realised that the theatre brought together the skills of the artisan and the creativity of the artist and that theatre craft melded together almost all the Settlement's activities into one cohesive whole.

At a National Council of Social Services Easter School at Leeds in 1935, Sir Percy Watkins said, "I think I see in the enforced idleness of all our thousands of decent, able people, unexpected opportunities of doing something that our educational leaders have hitherto not visualised very clearly. We have, at this moment, opportunities in our clubs of providing for quite an appreciable proportion of our adult populations, simple and informal kinds of education, suited to their individual experience of life, congenial to their interests, and in close affinity with their aptitudes. I submit, for instance, when a man is engaged upon making a chair under sound instruction, with all that it implies in knowledge of different kinds of timber, in careful measurements, in skilled handling of the appropriate tools and in the proper treatment of the medium, that something is happening, not only to a piece of wood, but also to a man's mind and personality. Rightly conceived, such a process as this can be a most valuable form of education." This 'form of education' was regularly practised at the Spennymoor Settlement and was a vital and valid part of its ethos during the 1930s.

chapter four

The Sketching Club

Tom Alderson, Bill Farrell, Bob Heslop & Bert Dees (Seated)

Bill Farrell believed in the efficacy of the 'rub it out and do it again' school of art

The other group in the field of creative art that Bill Farrell had introduced with the opening of the Spennymoor Settlement was the Sketching Club. Unlike the Theatre Group, the Sketching Club received no formal tuition and learning was by mutual criticism and encouragement. The Club was initiated by Bert Dees, a painter and decorator by trade, whose knowledge of the potential of paint as a medium was acknowledged by Bill Farrell as being second to none. Of the other five original members only two were miners. The basic principle upon which this Club was created was originality – there was strictly no copying of existing works. This teaching method was somewhat at odds with the established principles of copying 'old masters' and casts of classical sculpture, proof positive that much of Bill Farrell's vision was quite radical.

The members drew directly from life using models for portraiture and life drawing and they would go out into the countryside to test their powers of observation. Without the usual kind of academic tuition, painting simply because they wanted to paint, thrashing out problems of technique in argument, criticising and encouraging one another, the Sketching Club attained significant standing as a serious art group. The Club believed in the efficacy of the trial and error method of practice and the 'rub it out and do it again' technique!

Norman Cornish - Eddy's Fish Shop, Mixed Media

In 1933 the Club held its first exhibition which was to become an annual event and was dubbed in the press by the misnomer 'The Miners' Academy'. Subsequent exhibitions became known by the equally misleading title of 'The Pitman's Academy', for of the six exhibitors only one, Robert John Heslop, was a working miner and none of the pictures in this exhibition were of industrial or mining scenes. In all there were over one hundred and fifty items on display which included drawings and designs, needlework, carpentry and other craft work. In reviewing the 1933 exhibition the Northern Echo said, "An artist is not a man who can copy any existing work but someone who is moved by the creative spirit to work out his own artistic ideals and impressions. It is upon this basis that the club has been reared." From the beginning of the Settlement the Sketching Club was the only group that was allowed to sell its work, the reason being that its activities in no way impinged upon the livelihood of any other member of the local community.

Bill Farrell held the perception that the level of appreciation of art in the community was that of a 'pretty picture', exemplifying this by saying, "Most people in Spennymoor today still believe that a person who can make a pencil drawing of a stag at bay is the only true artist! And people have been known to stand in front of our pictures on exhibition and exclaim 'By, it's like a real picture!' The emphasis is on the real." The Club's progress in experiential art, as promulgated by Bill Farrell, can be judged by submissions in the 1935 exhibition, many of which illustrated the drabness of industrialisation. Bert Dees depicted dilapidated pit headgear in his work, an unconventional topic at the time, but it was his painting entitled 'Slag Lane', illustrating rows of humble cottages in the heart of a Spennymoor dominated by its Town Hall and the defunct Weardale Iron Works and slag heaps, that epitomised the reality of the life in the Spennymoor of this period.

"At this time," Bill Farrell tells us, "the real purpose of art in society was lost and had become overladen with purely aesthetic arguments about beauty." He believed and promoted the notion, "... the artist can only successfully paint those things that attract him most strongly and those are invariably things with which he lives and either loves or hates fiercely." He

Tom McGuinness - Domino Players, Charcoal 1949

advocated painting from direct experience and this advice was later to influence the subject matter of the Settlement's two most prominent artists – Norman Cornish and Tom McGuinness, both of whom were miners and both of whom progressed to create unique bodies of work documenting the coal miner's life – Norman Cornish in his scenes of the social life of the miner and the people of his home town of Spennymoor and Tom McGuinness in his atmospheric portrayal of conditions underground.

In a subsequent radio broadcast made by Bill Farrell he was able to report that much of the innate restraint that had inhibited the Sketching Club members initially had been overcome by his influence. "...Gradually, slowly, we broke away from self-consciousness, both in the manner of painting and in the painting itself. ...Artists are affected by everything that surrounds them and if they are citizens of Spennymoor must be affected by the things, the people and the conditions of Spennymoor. But they are gifted with one more language than is possessed by most of their fellows for they can speak with paint as well as with words."

He went on to say, "It is a gift to be used in the service of others...that service can best be given in, at and about the time and place the artist lives. Well then, the county, the life and people of Durham and Spennymoor are almost unknown to people outside the area and all are the poorer for lack of knowledge...To us these things are Durham people, places and scenes and ideally they should, and we do hope will, reflect the hopes and aspirations of all those other less gifted inarticulate ones who make up the majority of our Durham neighbours…With strength of purpose our group knows its place in society, explains something of why its members continue to paint and will, upon reflection, show a little of what painting does to the individual artist. Our group came together during the bad days of unemployment. It got a sense of purpose and service and perhaps because of that, later improved economic conditions did not cause interest to drop. It was just the reverse in fact…" The Sketching Club met on Wednesdays and Saturdays in winter and by mutual consent in summer.

Norman Cornish - Colliery & Streets, Oil Sketch

The media reinforced Bill Farrell's observations when it reported on the 1936 exhibition, "To try to restore some of the colour which industrialisation has driven from everyday life, that is the object of the workman artists of Spennymoor. There are six of them. They have lived in the shadow of the pitheads all their lives but why shouldn't a miner be able to paint with sympathy and understanding? These men do and allied to their natural talent is a brave spirit of enthusiasm. That spirit is the secret of the success of the Spennymoor Settlement to which they belong." [Sunday Sun 22nd March 1936]. The reporter had visited the Settlement and his eye was caught by "…a vivid and arresting watercolour of Spennymoor. I felt that the artist had striven in this symbolic work to express the grimmer aspects of the machine age. There was poetry in his handiwork. He had taken Spennymoor's dishevelled sky-line and modelled it into an eloquent and touching appeal." Sadly the reporter omits to identify the artist or the painting.

chapter five

The Members' Association

Children's Play Centre (Photo courtesy of Durham University Library)

"The children literally staggered home with their sacks
on their backs and contentment in their hearts."

Dorothy Martin

Whilst the 'cultural' aspect of the Settlement's activities is well documented and perhaps represents its greatest legacy, the more mundane social aspects of Settlement life may well have been the cohesive element which underpinned the longevity and success of the Spennymoor Settlement. Much of this is not documented and does not appear in Bill Farrell's annual reports. Fortunately, minute books from the Members' Association remain to advise us of the myriad of social and recreational activities taking place during the 1930s. These events ranged from whist-drives to rambles, from pie and pea suppers to Halloween dances. As long-time Settlement member William Mason records "…The committee [of the Members' Association] seems to have seized every opportunity of arranging such gatherings. As the

The Spennymoor Settlement

Hallowe'en Party, 1976

Members' Association was responsible for organising social activities, so it was also responsible for financing them: and as many of the members were unemployed it was not considered extraordinary for the treasurer to report to the Annual General Meeting that the balance in hand was 5d!"

From its inception the Settlement encouraged all comers. In the first year it enrolled over two hundred and fifty men and women and over one hundred children. The Children's Play Centre began in 1932 and continued until 1942. It was run by Mina (Wilhelmina) Martin, a teacher from Durham, who was encouraged to take up the post by her sister Dorothy who was already running the Girls' Club and later was to organise a Women's Group. The Children's Play Centre was open for an hour every Saturday morning and attracted children

Christmas Party

of all ages. Mina recalls that it began in a primitive way: a small brick hut and no equipment other than a band of willing helpers - toys began to be collected, dolls' clothing was knitted by the older girls and the boys improvised toys using odd scraps of materials. "Every Saturday morning came the patter of little feet and the chatter of many voices as the lane became thronged with eager children. They had but one breathless question 'Is the Settlement on?' ...What then," she asks in the Settlement's 21st birthday magazine of 1951, "attracted these children? The opportunity, for one short hour, to express themselves freely, to play with others

Dorothy & Mina Martin (Photo courtesy of Rene Chaplin)

or to play alone, to explore and experiment; to appeal for help and to know that help would be forthcoming." The numbers attending greatly increased with the evacuation of Tyneside children to Spennymoor and surrounding villages at the outbreak of the Second World War. This, however, had a positive gain, in that professional nursery help was available with the arrival of a Miss Craven who was able to borrow nursery equipment from the Bensham Settlement. Thus a separate Nursery Group was established as this play equipment became available – a particular delight for Betty Farrell who was herself a trained nursery teacher. As early as 1936 the Settlement had played host to a touring exhibition organised partly by the Nursery Schools Association. This exhibition acknowledged the need for nursery education and recognised its value, despite the reluctance of local authorities to venture into its provision. The Spennymoor Settlement was enlightened in supporting the concept of education for the under fives.

Santa Claus has been!

The yearly high point for the children was the Christmas party. Toys came from a Guide Company in the south. Volunteers at the Settlement spent a week carefully selecting and wrapping an individual sack of Christmas gifts which were carefully chosen with each particular child in mind. "The children literally staggered home with their sacks on their backs and contentment in their hearts," recalls Mina Martin. Her sister Dorothy remembers the excitement of the Christmas party held in the stone floored hut. "There was the noise of the sledge and the bells ringing …the off noises were provided by Jack Maddison … as he [Father Christmas/Bill Farrell] came in. What I remember most about it was the silence … There was dead silence and just a terrific sense of wonderment when Father Christmas arrived."

Sub-warden Jack Maddison began a successful Scout Troup although it did have its early difficulties. "At one period it had to share quarters with the Theatre Group. Later the Players moved on to another place and the hut took on its more dignified and functional role of Scout Hut, where brains and bodies could be (and were) strewn about the floor, without the added fatigue of sweeping up so that another group could use the place. On one occasion the Scouts were unable to use the Hut and had to meet in the Theatre. They manfully strove to make the best of what to them was a very bad job. They were greatly surprised when the Warden was not prostrate with gratitude at the way they held their meetings."

Bill Farrell, who was nominally the Scout Master, ensured that even the scouts were involved in back stage work for theatre productions. In the seminal production 'Distant Point' in 1942, the Scouts played a vital role in assisting with two big scene changes. Everyone was given a particular task and woe betide anyone who made a mistake. The Scouts rose to the occasion and the play was considered by Bill Farrell to be the best production up to that date. One of the leading lights in this production was housewife Carrie Johnson, the wife of a Durham miner. She was representative of most working class women of the time – dominated by her husband and subsumed by the daily grind of washing and cooking and caring for her family. "There's an old saying in the coal fields, 'Better be a skivvy than a pitman's wife,' Carrie herself tells us. "I have to sit and reckon up at the week-end and arrange my work and recreation for each different shift. As for meals – try to plan a substantial meal for a very hungry man who comes in at 11.30pm and is going straight to bed (oh, his indigestion!), or a meal at 2.30am before he goes out on a winter's morning." The Settlement offered her a means of escape from this

Jack Maddison helps out (Photo courtesy of Rene Chaplin)

Cast of 'The Corn is Green' 1952

31

life of drudgery and she was able to forget her everyday life and reinvent herself on stage. She is singled out for special mention in the review of 'The Corn is Green' by Emlyn Williams in December 1952. "Carrie Johnson's erstwhile light-fingered Cockney turned militantly righteous housekeeper was nicely balanced between character and caricature and provided much laughter." Carrie was well liked by all and was to be a great help and support to Bill Farrell in the dark days of the 1950s.

chapter six

The Everyman Players

Betty Farrell in 'Hedda Gabler' 1940

"…Voice production is most important for one has to get people to speak intelligibly and with the minimum of effort. Again, however, there is a danger for one must not eradicate the local peculiarities despite the fact that most people who want to ACT also wish to speak the bastardised flat English of the upper middle class. There are such snobs in all walks of life."

Unlike the Sketching Club which had no direct tuition, the Theatre Group had specific teaching on stagecraft from Bill Farrell. He also used play rehearsals as an opportunity to expand on social and political teaching. "It is necessary to know just what a character's social, political and religious background is before one can get to grips with him. A character portrayed on stage must be a person who has a history before his appearance on the stage and who will have a life after he has made his final exit… I defy anybody to work in a real theatre without adding to his knowledge. Our theatre has never been thought of as a place where amateurs play. It's a place where a real job has to be done by actors, poets, painters, singers, dancers, carpenters, electricians and seamstresses."

"Its value to the individual is so enormous that it just can't be measured. Theatre practice as an artist gives one back to oneself. It gives control. It gives confidence. The hesitant shuffler who can't get himself out of a room learns to take command of such a situation and his hands and feet no longer wiggle about like legs of mutton on a butcher's bar – they belong to him and obey him. One man – one of our pitmen – joined the Theatre Company with a seemingly incurable stammer. Well it has been almost completely cured for him by voice production exercises with the Theatre Company and by giving him private tuition in another language. He has even been able to play the leading role in 'Everyman'. That man's story is just a part of the story of the Spennymoor Settlement."

"It is the rule of the company," Bill Farrell explained in his eighth annual report of 1939, "that each and every member of the [Theatre Group] shall be first and foremost a theatre-craftsman, and only then a potential actor or actress. The dilettante, suburban-mannequin parade kind of actor or actress is not encouraged." Teacher Dorothy Martin, responsible for running the Girls' Club, recalled, "It is no accident that my most vivid recollections of the theatre are concerned with production rather than with acting … I served my apprenticeship in every department – props, promoter, assistant stage manager and assistant electrician. In the latter capacity I helped to install the stage electrical system and learned that fitting innumerable fuses is not an honour to be sought but a 'dirty job' always delegated to the electrician's second mate."

The impact that Bill Farrell's ethos had on theatre craft can be illustrated by the experience and subsequent career of Settlement member Edith Kirtley's brother-in-law, John Murray, an engineer who had been drafted to work in the munitions factory at Spennymoor in 1941. Sitting in a local pub one evening wondering where the next digs were coming from, his companion Mitchell McKenzie, a commercial artist from Scotland, pronounced that there must better things to do in the evenings than waste time. Thus they tried the Settlement on an evening when by chance a new play was being cast. Bill Farrell was delighted to welcome prospective male members.

John recalled, "He [Bill Farrell] took us on one side and told us the aims of the Settlement and then went across the back yard to open a door to paradise … he showed us the amenities of the stage which probably was the best equipped between Spennymoor and the Theatre Royal, Newcastle upon Tyne … For Mitchell McKenzie and myself the Settlement became our second home and for myself I took part in several productions as an actor sometimes helping behind stage." On returning to Manchester after the war John was inspired to join a dramatic society and it was not long before the training he had absorbed at the Settlement encouraged him to produce plays and teach drama. Mitchell McKenzie went on to design stage sets for the Settlement, most notably 'They Came to the City', which was staged in 1945 and for which some of his original designs still exist today.

John Murray's first-hand account of Bill Farrell's stagecraft methods gives us a great insight into Bill's exacting, yet inspirational, teaching techniques. "We might spend a whole evening on two

John Murray as Joe Dinmore & Pat French as Alice in J.B. Priestley's 'They Came to a City', 1945

pages and during that time Bill Farrell would put us into various situations, moving the characters about, giving us the opportunity of acting another part, perhaps leading off into several exercises of how to enter or exit successfully, pausing on the line, throwing one away, becoming various characters. His biggest teaching vehicle was that of priming two actors in several pieces of dialogue and allowing the rest of us to try and guess what relationship they were, who they were, what the situation was and then putting it to the actors later that they had got across something and how had it come across. It would be analysed until late in the evening and the rehearsal resumed the following week."

Similarly, Edith Kirtley who joined in 1941 made her acting debut in June 1944 in the single-act play 'The Sword and the Spirit' by R. Swingler and remained an active member and indeed ultimately President of the Settlement prior to her death in 2007. Recalling her experiences in 'Homespun', Edith commented on how she had benefited from Bill's professional knowledge. She had been involved with the Methodist Church and already had a keen interest in music and drama. "I learned to read plays, not just

Cradle Song, 1934

at surface level but phrase by phrase and sometimes word by word, seeking the right meaning and intonation, bringing shape and depth to the work. From him I learned to appreciate fine acting and sets, effects and lighting …" Indeed Edith became not only an extremely fine actress but an inspiring and technically exacting producer in her own right.

The Theatre Group (The Settlement Community Players) began with a small group of women, mainly miners' wives, who established a Play Reading Group – the first group to be established within the Settlement. "The women pleaded for a play to break down the drabness of their existence and to give expression to their feelings," said Bill Farrell. Their first public performance, Sierras' three-act comedy 'Cradle Song', did not take place until 13th October 1934. It was in rehearsal for a full year and all but three parts were played by women. The Warden noted in his annual report, "Artistically it proved beyond our wildest expectations, and as it produced a profit of £20 it was sound financially." The Northern Echo in its review stated, "… [Cradle Song] represents an endeavour to sustain one more cultural activity at a time when uncouth banalities and great economic distress seem to be stifling all that is best in human nature." The Group's second production, Synge's 'Playboy of the Western World', was performed in St Andrew's Mission Hall. Reviews of the play extolled the performance of Bill Farrell who also directed and acclaimed teacher Ann Hodgson's portrayal of Pageen. (Ann Hodgson was eventually to become the wife of Fritz Hess and move to London but she remained in contact with the Farrells throughout. In a letter to Bill Farrell in 1947 when Settlement funding was becoming precarious due to the withdrawal of support by The Pilgrim Trust, Ann revealed that her wealthy German husband whose first wife, Tisa Hess, had designed the sculpture on the outside of the Settlement building, would not contribute to Settlement funds as he perceived Bill Farrell as having communist sympathies).

As William Mason, author of a study into adult education and the Settlement Movement records, "From these small beginnings the Settlement Players developed into one of the finest amateur companies in the North of England reaching its zenith in the war years with an ambitious production of the Russian play, 'Distant Point' by Alexander Afinogenyev." In a subsequent radio broadcast, 'Art for Everyone', Bill Farrell confirmed that 'Distant Point' had been "…our best production so far …this play dealt with a small community isolated in the wilds of the far east of the USSR amongst whom was a young man who was dissatisfied with life in the wilds. He wanted to go to Moscow but a chance visit from an Army General who was dying of an incurable disease, but who yet thought of his country first, brought the young malcontent to realise that however small and however useless it may seem, if it is service for the great and common cause it is just as important as is the service of the highest in the land. Our Company has since heard two broadcasts of that play, but I'm not sure our own production didn't get nearer to the author's ideal, because after all our actors are all working class people with REAL working class voices, beliefs and aspirations. We believe in the plays we do or we wouldn't do them!"

William Mason acknowledges the benefits he gained from attending the W.E.A. classes at the Settlement following his demobilisation from the forces in 1947 and the influence that the Settlement, which he refers to as 'Everyman's University', had upon his personal development. He returned to his pre-war apprenticeship as a coach painter with a local firm of coach builders, attending Sub-Warden Jack Maddison's classes in his free time. After three years study he achieved an Adult Exhibition awarded by Durham County Education Committee. This gave him the opportunity to enter Ruskin College, Oxford, in October 1950. After studying there for two years William took the Oxford University Diploma in Economics and Political Science, moving to Oriel College, Oxford, in October 1952, to read modern history, from where he graduated with honours. Ultimately William obtained a Diploma in Education from St. Cuthbert's Society, Durham, before embarking on a teaching career. In homage to the work of Bill Farrell, he made the Residential Settlement Movement the subject of his dissertation, with particular reference to the work of the Spennymoor Settlement.

'Distant Point' a topical Soviet play, was performed as the high point of the Festival of Art at the Settlement which took place during the whole of June 1942. Bill Farrell exclaimed in his diary of the time, "A most marvellous week! ...Not all of us will live to see the coming events ... that will surely arise as a result of this production of a real Peoples' play by and in a real Peoples' theatre." In his 12th Annual Report 1942 – 1943, referring to the play, Bill Farrell wrote, "The event

Betty Farrell & Dorothy Martin (Photo courtesy of Rene Chaplin)

was indeed a revelation of the power and purpose of the theatre when allied to the Social Sciences and has convinced many people here once and for all, that what we have been laboriously teaching and preaching for many years was true. Last summer the Spennymoor Settlement was on the crest of a wave of creative enthusiasm. It has not died down yet and we still get echoes of its effect on the general public when we hear and talk about it still even in the pits. The spiritual experience and the knowledge gained will remain with us for ever." Writing with hindsight, John Murray suggests it was no coincidence that this play about nationalism in Russia had been chosen for production in 1942. Since 1941 the German offensive had changed and now was aimed firmly at Russia. The Royal Ordnance Factory in Spennymoor was manufacturing munitions which were being shipped via the Northern Passage to the war-beleaguered Soviets. In selecting this play perhaps Bill Farrell was revealing, like many others of the time, his sympathies with the socialist aims of communism.

The opening of the Everyman Theatre, March 29th 1939

The Festival programme details those who were involved with the production, many of whom already were or were to become stalwart members of the Settlement. These included cast members Norman Cornish who played Sulin, ADC to the General - his only recorded acting role - Carrie Johnson as Glasha, Betty Farrell as Vera and George Roantree as Koriushka. (George Roantree, sometimes referred to as 'Rowntree'' was to return to act with the Everyman Players in 1968 after an absence of over twenty years and played the porter in 'Doctor in the House' to rave reviews – testimony to the affection George felt for the Settlement). The production team consisted of Dorothy Martin as assistant producer, with lighting and stage management by Jack Maddison (assisted by J. Welch, R. Outhwaite, F. Phillips and G. Trotter), sets painted by W. Ratcliff, Mitchell Mackenzie and Bert Dees. Costumes were the responsibility of the Sub-Warden's wife, Mary Maddison, and Mina Martin was the properties mistress and the business manager was Magnus Pearson. The importance of the Theatre and theatre craft to the ethos of the Settlement can be inferred from the fact that virtually all those involved in this seminal production had other major roles within the Settlement's curriculum, yet it was the theatre that gave cohesion to the organisation.

The Group had realised that, to develop, it required a permanent theatre of its own. In 1935 the Settlement was awarded a grant from the Special Government Commission for Depressed Areas towards altering and extending the existing premises and building a theatre. Government money totalled £1250, conditional upon the Settlement raising the remaining £262. The money was acquired from a variety of sources in ingenious ways. Some came from the Special Commissioner, some from old professional theatre friends of Bill Farrell and some from the women members and local friends and supporters. "The women were really marvellous. They were the best money raisers because they weren't afraid to do it in the small ways … some even made toffee at home and sold it for a penny a bag so that they could have a theatre of their own."

The theatre, built to the design of Charles Elgey, was opened on the 29th March 1939 by George Gillett, Commissioner for the Distressed Areas. This was followed by tea in the library and, at 5.00pm, a performance of 'Everyman' – the 500-year-old morality play - with a cast of over 20 and after which the theatre company was to take its name. The colourful mediaeval costumes had been made by the Sewing and Theatre Groups, based on Bill Farrell's designs. (Bill was meticulous in his preparations, obtaining copies of portraits from the National Portrait Gallery to ensure the authenticity

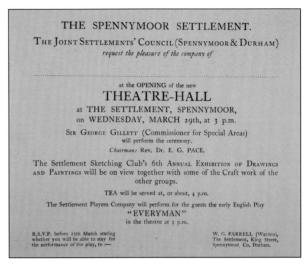

THE SPENNYMOOR SETTLEMENT.

The Joint Settlements' Council (Spennymoor & Durham)
request the pleasure of the company of

at the OPENING of the new

THEATRE-HALL

at THE SETTLEMENT, SPENNYMOOR,
on WEDNESDAY, MARCH 29th, at 3 p.m.

Sir George Gillett (Commissioner for Special Areas)
will perform the ceremony.
Chairman: Rev. Dr. E. G. PACE.

The Settlement Sketching Club's 6th Annual Exhibition of Drawings and Paintings will be on view together with some of the Craft work of the other groups.

TEA will be served at, or about, 4 p.m.

The Settlement Players Company will perform for the guests the early English Play
"EVERYMAN"
in the theatre at 5 p.m.

R.S.V.P. before 15th March stating whether you will be able to stay for the performance of the play, to —

W. G. FARRELL (Warden),
The Settlement, King Street,
Spennymoor, Co. Durham.

Invitation to the opening of the theatre

Building the Everyman Theatre

Laying the foundations for the Everyman Theatre

of the costumes). The theatre is tiny, seating approximately 80 patrons (although the sign still extant in the theatre states that it was originally licensed to accommodate 120 persons) and in its day provided the most up to date and advanced equipment available. As with the Sketching Club, members would not make do and it was equipped with everything the most exacting producer could desire.

"Bill Farrell introduced Spennymoor to the work of O'Casey, Priestley, Strindberg, Ibsen, Gorky and a host of others. A first night at the theatre attracted national attention. On the opening night of Strindberg's 'Easter', his English biographer, Elizabeth Sprigge, marvelled at a mining community's response to this sensitive playwright,"

Caravan City with George Shiels and Jack Maddison

enthused Arnold Hadwin. During the Second World War performances by visiting concert artists organised by the Council for the Encouragement of Music and the Arts, later to become the Arts Council, took place as well as visits from professional touring theatre companies, including The Old Vic which, directed by Tyrone Guthrie, performed 'The Merchant of Venice' in 1941.

Bill Farrell, searching for plays which would suit his basically working class Company and which his audience would understand, whilst at the same time bearing some relation to their lives and hopes and aspirations, began to train dramatists and to experiment with the

Robert Heslop's set design for 'Everyman', Watercolour

group-writing of plays. Sid Chaplin, one of the most famous and notable of the Settlement members, received much encouragement and constructive criticism from Bill Farrell in his early attempts at playwriting. Settlement member George Shiels was also to emerge as a playwright

Cast of Everyman, 1939 (Photo courtesy of Durham University Library)

Cast of 'The New Gossoon' by George Shiels, November 1946

and three of his plays, 'The New Gossoon',' The Caretaker' and 'Quinn's Secret' were performed by the company between 1946 and 1951. George Shiels had kept a diary from 4th January to 3rd October 1937 whilst he had been a machine gunner in the Spanish Civil War with the International Brigade. This diary was later used by poet and academic Sir Stephen Spender when he was compiling a history of the International Brigade, based on eye-witness accounts. Sadly there is no sign of the embryonic writer's diary today but its creation demonstrates that even whilst under the greatest duress, George felt compelled to write. Membership of the Settlement allowed and encouraged him to develop his talent.

chapter seven

The Pitman's Academy

Hanging the exhibition (Photo courtesy of Durham University Library)

"Arts should portray the present in the light of the past, and the future in the light of both, and hopes for the future based upon the knowledge of what is possible"

The Pitman's Academy was the misnomer with which the press had dubbed the Sketching Club. It was first used in 1934. The Herald on June 24th 1933 had previously made reference to the Miner's Academy in connection with the Settlement's first exhibition. This exhibition comprised over 150 items – including needlework, carpentry and other craft work, in addition to paintings by the then six members of the Sketching Club. Of these six members two – Arthur Hawkins and J. Jones – were unemployed miners, Robert (Bob) John Heslop was a working miner employed at the Dean and Chapter Colliery, Ferryhill, Herbert (Bert) Bewick Dees was a painter and decorator, George Warren's situation is not documented and the sixth member of the group was the Warden of the Settlement himself – Bill Farrell. Although the constituency of the membership of the Sketching Club fluctuated over the years, it was never exclusively a club for miners, but the name stuck.

Norman Cornish - Bar Scene, Pastel

As was the case with the Ashington Group which would appear some three years later, there was to be no formal tuition in the practical skills of painting and drawing. The two groups differed in their aims at inception in that the Spennymoor men were interested in the practice of art whereas initially the Ashington men were concerned with art appreciation. As Bill Farrell explained, "without the usual kind of academic tuition, painting simply because we want to, thrashing out problems of technique together in argument, criticising one another, delighting in our progress, we have attained some standing as serious workers in the pictorial arts."

The men were serious about their art and strictly adhered to Bill Farrell's insistence that they use only top quality materials, "…we were able as a group to make bulk purchases of the best artist's materials – never student's materials. Somehow, even in the hardest times, our Sketching Club has managed to get the best and we have never had to compromise with making do. That doesn't mean that we are spendthrifts, that would go against the very grain of Durham character. We've used cardboard instead of canvas and one elderly ex-miner, Jack Evans, a quiet, gentle man has been seen in the early days carefully putting back in tubes all the unused paint off his palette."

Both Bert Dees and Bob Heslop had received some art tuition from accomplished amateur artist Jack Evans [1871 – 1967]. Although Jack had been a miner in the Spennymoor area he did not paint mining scenes and, whilst proficient in a wide range of media and being widely read about art, he never became a regular member of the Sketching Club. Despite, or maybe because, there was no formal art tuition at the Sketching Club the men's thirst for information was unassuaged. They made great use of the public library which was housed in the Settlement and administered by Betty Farrell to extend their technical knowledge and to widen their awareness of the works of the Great Masters. Settlement members Sid Chaplin, Norman Cornish, Bob Heslop and Tom McGuinness in particular have all paid great tribute to the opportunity offered by this free service.

As well as being serious about the quality of their materials, the members were equally serious about the originality of their work. Men tested their powers of observation by drawing directly from nature or from life models. The manner of their work widened to depict all forms of local life including derelict pit heaps and mean back streets. Referring to the Spennymoor Settlement's

Bill Farrell - Abstract, Oil

1935 exhibition, The North East Daily Gazette of 27th November, reported, "the painting section which is the largest in the exhibition, although representative of that of a numerically small group, is extremely good and well worth the trouble of a visit …The progress of the artists is revealed by the way they are now able to make an artistic design from the old pit heads which are not noted for their beauty …As a centre for craftsmanship and culture the Settlement will repay a visit during the next three days."

This was reinforced by an article in the Durham County Advertiser of the same day, "once again there was an outstanding display of the oil paintings, watercolours and sketches of a small circle of local artists which includes three miners. They have picked out many corners illustrating the drabness of industrialisation and the natural beauty of the woods and the riverside, so much so that it is difficult to believe the one is within a stone's throw of the other and not in an adjoining country." Thus, within a mere four years of its inception, the Club had found inspiration in the industrial scene as a valid subject for its art.

Robert Heslop - Lake District, Oil, 1930s

The initial motive force behind the creation of the Sketching Club seems to have been Bert Dees who was the first to join Bill Farrell's Club and was already an accomplished artist, being the only amateur artist to have had work exhibited at the Laing Art Gallery, Newcastle, in 1927. Bert Dees was a native Tynesider, being born in Newcastle in 1892, one of a family of artists. His brother John Arthur Dees, some eighteen years the senior, studied at Gateshead School of Art and was a Royal Academician. Bert and his family had moved to Spennymoor during its boom years when he was six years old. He had served in the PALS regiment during the Great War and after the armistice he set up a business as a household painter and decorator in which he worked until his retirement at the age of seventy. The generous nature of the man can be judged from the fact that he gave one of his paintings as a Christmas present to every customer whose house he had decorated that year. Bert Dees recollected a conversation with one of his customers, an elderly landlord whose property he had been painting all week. "Thank God its Saturday dinner time!" I said …as I began to put away ladders, steps, paint and brushes, the old man said, 'If a wes thoo aad wark this afterneun an' git the job finished seein' its sech a fine day.' "No fear," said I "we go out sketching every Saturday afternoon." 'Skitchin' he said, 'what kind ova gee-em is that?' I explained to him that a group of men – young and old – met on Saturday afternoons at the Settlement Sketching Club and, armed with watercolours and paper, or oil colours and canvases, went off into the woods, down to the River Wear, or to any part of the nearby countryside and, after admiring the beauty of the trees, cottages and bridges, would decide on a suitable composition and try to paint a picture from it. 'Aa think thoos aal wastin' yer time an' trouble. Why man aa hear ye can buy picters for few coppers at the auction sales and onyway the missus tellt me that picters have gone out of fashion'. And with that parting shot he went into his house slamming the door after him." Presumably this customer didn't appreciate his Christmas present!

While recalling this incident Bert reflected, "Wall pictures may have gone out of fashion in some quarters, but the joy of painting them has certainly not. The fellowship created by a Sketching Group, the friendly comradeship, and the discussions and the arguments of this and that school of painting, when Picasso and Henry Moore, Munnings and Minton, Van Gogh and Cezanne are glorified, criticised and often damnified, is a very real pleasure and is constructive. Members help each other with paint, brushes or paper, and advice. Of course, there is friendly rivalry but we think that is a sure sign of a healthy group."

Viewing the Pitman's Academy. 1936 (Newspaper cutting, courtesy of The Northern Echo)

Bill Farrell described Bert as, "A very real artist and a first grade craftsman who loved and understood the tools with which he worked. He used them assiduously and often produced work with that little known spiritual quality known as art…he is a man who knows more about paint and what it will do than many others in his profession…He lives to paint and perhaps even paints in his sleep! He'd been painting pictures more or less surreptitiously for years. In a mining town like Spennymoor a painter has to work surreptitiously or be thought mad in these days. But going out as a group gave the Sketching Club great moral support and slowly the sight of a grown man sitting down drawing in a public place when he might have been at a football match grew less and less queer in the eyes of Spennymoor."

Bert has been described as a traditionalist in his work. His original subject matter was mainly landscape and still life. Although never tempted to practise 'modern art' he was widely read in the current art trends and whilst appreciating modernist movements including the experimental work of the Bauhaus pioneers in Germany, it was not for him. Bert and the rest of the Sketching Club members had direct exposure to the work of the Bauhaus School of Art, Berlin, in their 1935 exhibition which included abstract studies exhibited by Jos Thain. Jos who came from South Shields had been trained at the Bauhaus under Paul Klee and Kandinsky and was back in England after the expulsion of the School following the advent of the Nazi regime. " … The progress of the artists is revealed by the way they are now able to make an artistic design from the old pit heads which are not noted for their beauty. Mr Bert Dees has one or two well-executed pictures on this subject and he is of course strongly represented in the show … Even more

Herberrt Dees - Autumn, Waterclour, 1961

Herbert Dees - Slag Lane, Oil, 1935

controversial will be the attention paid to Mr Jos Thain's abstract studies. ... He belongs to one of the most advanced modern schools of painting and the fact that four of his paintings are on view at the Settlement for three days of the exhibition – Thursday, Friday and Saturday – will attract many practising artists to the exhibition. As a centre for craftsmanship and culture the Settlement will repay a visit during the next three days." [North East Daily Gazette 27th November 1935].

Although known as a landscape painter, in that same 1935 exhibition, Bert Dees had contributed his striking work showing the depressed areas entitled 'Slag Lane'. The depressive air in the brooding oil painting is accentuated by the formless masses of the waste heaps and the thick pall of smoke above the mean dwellings and the derelict Iron Works. He continued the theme of dereliction when, in the 1936 annual exhibition Bert went on to exhibit small tempera and watercolour studies of abandoned industrial workings around Spennymoor which the Northern Echo saw as examples of " ...the artist's practised eye finding pleasure and unexpected beauty in the abandoned workings," whilst other critics construed these as satirical comments on Durham life. Despite these examples of social commentary Bert remained a landscape painter at heart. In spite of favourable reviews, Jos Thain's fortunes waned in later years and letters exist between him and Bill Farrell, dated November and December 1955, enquiring about the

Robert Heslop - Dean & Chapter, Watercolour, 1963

possibility of showing some of his work at the Settlement. He offers to loan the paintings out on payment of a small fee and also suggests selling on a hire purchase basis as he cannot afford to buy equipment to paint nor to purchase canvases.

The other mainstay of the early years of the Sketching Club was Bob Heslop [1907 – 1988], a putter at Dean and Chapter Colliery, Ferryhill. The colliery owner's commitment to miners' safety was demonstrated when the pit manager asked a young Bob Heslop to illustrate pit safety rules after seeing his life-like chalk drawings of workmates on roadway walls. The resultant series of posters, displayed in the lamp cabin at the colliery, may well have been the first health and safety posters in industrial Britain. During the war years he designed an award-winning poster depicting coal tubs on a pair of scales displaying the slogan, 'That last tub may swing the scales of victory'. Norman Cornish would later recognise Bob's flair for design by describing his posters as inspired and well crafted. It is perhaps not surprising that Bob became a highly proficient screen print maker, a medium which lends itself beautifully to poster work.

Bob was a local man, born in Spennymoor's Dundas Street and attended Rosa Street School. One of six brothers he briefly worked for the London and Newcastle Tea Company before entering the local collieries where he was to spend the next forty two years. Watercolour was Bob Heslop's forte. "Coming out of darkness and scratting about in fifteen to twenty inches of seam height his box and brushes became the keys of a kingdom of air and light and land. But look at his pastels, his silk screen work, and you will find gems of a differing order. He can work small as well as big; contrast the small pastels of Hill Top Farm with the …cool dispassionate treatment of Dean and Chapter Colliery his, and my, alma mater," so wrote Sid Chaplin in the introduction to an exhibition of Bob's work. Bob attended the Sketching Club regularly and exhibited consistently. As a result he sold many paintings which were sent to various parts of the country, including the headquarters of the Settlement Movement, Toynbee Hall and the National Coal Board offices in Hobart House, London. In the 1970s, he was commissioned by Durham County Council's Museum Service to document the headgear, past and present, of the mines of County Durham. Coal News of July 1973 reported that one of Bob's most intriguing tasks was to paint Westerton Colliery as it was. Using the rough sketches he had made in one of his many sketch books some forty years previously, Bob was delighted to be able to reconstruct a piece of mining history.

In 1939 both Bert Dees and Bob Heslop had work accepted for the Artists of the Northern Counties exhibition at the Laing Art Gallery Newcastle. As a first attempt Bob had submitted two paintings one in oils and the other a watercolour. The latter, entitled 'Old and New' – a view of the old worsted mill at Croxdale with a motorcar in the foreground - was accepted, a remarkable achievement and one which validated Bob's confidence in his own ability. He had reached the standard necessary for entry into this prestigious exhibition. One of his entries in the Settlement's 1941 exhibition was the subject of newspaper comment for his successful portrayal of the eerie

Robert Heslop - Bombardment, Watercolour, 1941

Norman Cornish - Grandmother, Charcoal

spectacle and stark realism of an industrial area undergoing bombardment. "Mr Heslop has reproduced with great fidelity the strange dawn-like effect of search light illumination at night and the yellow-red flashes of high explosives. In many senses this picture may become historic, it has certainly caught the atmosphere of nocturnal visits of bomb-carrying machines from enemy territory. It presents a somewhat gruesome scene that suggests all the horrors of the new type of terrorist warfare as practised by the Nazis."

In her 1942 article local journalist Elsie Robinson, commenting on the art produced by the Spennymoor Settlement Sketching Club, gives a stout defence of the validity of the Group's subject matter and prophetically advises on the future direction. "…[the artists] are living in a world of social upheaval; a world is at war; this area for twenty years has lived through a period approximating to war…the strain of hard, dangerous work, away from the light and sunshine and definite under-nourishment has produced men with faces that any artist should be proud to paint; hollow, gaunt faces of men who have yet the light of vision of the future in their eyes; women with pale, weary faces, hollow eyes, whose fingers are thickened and coarsened by the endless service that they only cease to render when those hands are permanently stilled. These should be the subjects of the Durham artists." (The young Norman Cornish in his powerful sketch of his grandmother, executed when he was a mere twenty years old, had pre-empted this perceptive analysis).

Elsie Robinson continued, "…An age of unrest, district of suffering, an industry seething with troubles and changes to come – and its artists only produce lovely landscapes and portraits. Leave that to the luckier south. If art has a purpose then it should be holding up a true glass to the people as they are now. It should be a stimulant to greater efforts for the production of a better life for miners and their families. Only a few exhibits reflect this true picture and one in particular, a crayon of the artist miner Victor Harding, shows one of the finest types of Durham Men: but there should be more. The Spennymoor Settlement Sketching Club has shown that it can match the masters of the past in skill; now let it show the present that it has a message that only it can give."

chapter eight

A slice of life

Norman Cornish - Bar Scene, Oil

"There is a universality of creative art
which defies time and place."

Norman Cornish

Norman Cornish is mentioned for the first time in Bill Farrell's Annual Report of 1936/37, the same report that states that, according to a Northern Echo article of the time, the Settlement's exhibitions are, "being considered of some importance in the art world and being visited by people from all over the British Isles." Bill Farrell singles out Norman Cornish for particular note in 1939 when he informs prophetically, "Some new members have joined all of whom show promise, but one young man in particular has shown of late a distinct talent for portraiture in oils. We expect much of him and only regret our inability to send him away to one of the larger

Schools of Art…a talent will not be wasted but it will take longer to come to fruition." Bill Farrell went on to comment, "Norman Cornish has painted portraits of his father and mother and of his grandmother, a fine old Durham woman with a characterful face which, if painted by a Rembrandt or Frans Hals, would tell the story of the Durham miners' wives for all the world to see." In the following year, 1940, Norman was to exhibit his first oil painting, a study of his sister Ella, in the Northern Counties exhibition in the Laing Art Gallery.

Norman Cornish - The Pit Road, Oil

Norman Cornish is undoubtedly the most celebrated artist to have attended the Settlement. He is now one of the most sought after contemporary artists in the country, with his large works easily commanding five figure sums. Norman is a Spennymoor man through and through. He was born on 18th November 1919 in Oxford Street, Spennymoor, where he lived until the family moved to Bishops Close Street, adjacent to the old ironworks and the gasworks. He shared the terraced house with his parents and his younger brothers Tom, Jack, Jim, Bobby, Billy and sister Ella and describes the housing conditions as primitive. It is not surprising perhaps that Norman was to contract diphtheria when he was seven.

Coalmining was thriving at Ferryhill some three miles to the south and many Spennymooor men were to tread the pit road through the allotments and across the fields to work - a pit road which was to provide the inspiration for several of Norman's mining images. When Norman was 14 his father was unemployed and, with the ambition of a college or university education thwarted, he left school and, like almost all his male contemporaries, he went to work as a coalminer in Dean and Chapter Colliery, Ferryhill.

All his life Norman has drawn and painted and his early memories influenced his lifelong passion for the local social scene and the street activities of the time - musicians and dancers, knife-grinders and street vendors plying their trade from horse-drawn carts - scenes which were to be reflected in his sketch books. Norman's working life began on Boxing Day in 1933 and his first job was as an underground datal lad. The unexpected, hectic but ordered activity of the colliery yard made an immediately deep impression on the youthful Norman, an impression that was to be permanently recorded in his art.

Norman had heard of the existence of a sketching club in Spennymoor but was not made immediately welcome at the Settlement. Indeed when he first arrived Bert Dees told the young Norman to go away and come back when he was fifteen. This Norman duly did and so became the Sketching Club's youngest member. Bert Dees took Norman under his wing, giving the eager newcomer much constructive advice. This gave Norman two foci to his life - work and art. The quality of Norman's work, particularly his portraiture, was quickly recognised both by Bill Farrell and the general public who were able to see the work of the Sketching Club in the eagerly anticipated annual exhibition. It was an appreciative admirer of his work, Mrs Baker-Baker who, having seen a drawing of the artist's grandmother, encouraged Norman to extend his range of media by giving him 10 guineas to buy oil paint. Mrs Baker-Baker was so impressed by the drawing that she felt it ought to be rendered in oil. Norman's first oil painting, however, was to be of his sister Ella.

Norman Cornish - Low Spennymoor, Watercolour

Norman Cornish - Old Elmore, Flomaster Pen

Norman was to work in the collieries – a reserved industry – throughout the Second World War. Immediately after the war he held his first one-man exhibition in the 'Green Room' at the People's Theatre in Newcastle upon Tyne. His first big break into the wider world of art, however, came in 1947 when Dr Reavans, the Director of Education for the newly formed National Coal Board, bought five of Norman's canvases and asked him to co-ordinate an exhibition, 'Art by the Miner' in London.

Norman continued to exhibit nationally whilst still remaining an active Sketching Club member. In 1950 he exhibited in the Artists' International Association Gallery near Leicester Square, London in 'The Coal Miners' - an exhibition which featured both professional artists such as Henry Moore and amateur mining artists – all displaying works on the common theme of the coalmine. At this time the Shipley Gallery in Gateshead continued its policy of holding exhibitions of contemporary art by local artists and Norman's work was regularly featured. In 1959 Norman first exhibited work in the Stone Gallery in St Mary's Place, Newcastle upon Tyne. This was to prove a fruitful liaison as the gallery actively promoted the work of artists with local connections. Among those featured were the Cumbrian artist Sheila Fell and Lancashire's Lawrence Stephen Lowry.

Norman's artistic record of the everyday life of his town – Spennymoor – is unsurpassed and as such his work is often likened to that of the Salford of Lowry. Both were loyal to their communities and expressed their versions of the effects of industrialisation. There the comparison should end. Lowry deliberately reduces his figures to an almost robotic depersonalisation – implying that industry dehumanises - rendering the characters into automata, with little evidence of a previous or subsequent life. Not so of Cornish. His subjects exude personality and are in close, even intimate, conversation, defying the economic hardships and oppressive circumstances of their plight. They laugh at, confide in, enjoy and relish each other's company. The viewer feels much more comfortable with Norman's friends than with Lowry's. Norman's canvas is, however, much wider and his images illustrate to us, the observers, a profound understanding of human behaviour and interaction; he is not merely chronicling life as he experienced it in a pit town but looking deeper into the visual relationships that constitute a society.

Norman Cornish - Detail from Gala Day, 1963.

The mellow, earthy tones of his finely veneered oils, the blended shades of his pastels, the comforting rounded forms of his principal characters and their interacting bodily positions, contrast starkly with our mental perceptions of the cold, forbidding clamour of the collier's lot - a lot that denied Norman a complete education but one that he has acutely observed, analysed and understood and that he has viewed with a warm and compassionate eye. His images - from the greatest oil painting to the smallest pen-drawn vignette - are keenly observed extracts from life and are the vehicles through which he educates us. Norman is a true artist, expressing his thoughts, feelings and philosophy in paint. At 88 years of age, Norman continues to chronicle the everyday world of the people of Spennymoor - his particular 'slice of life'.

Norman's appeal as an artist with a keen observational eye for the interpretation of the everyday activities of the mining communities was recognised in 1962 when he was commissioned to paint a 30-foot mural typifying life in County Durham for the new County Hall in Durham City. This building was a showpiece, a symbolic act of defiance by

Norman Cornish - Detail from Gala Day, 1963.

Norman Cornish - Detail from Gala Day, 1963.

a county whose livelihood was increasingly threatened by the escalating pit closures. The logistics of producing the mural were enormous - the locating of an extra-long canvas and the finding of a sufficiently large room proved problematical. Norman was granted unpaid leave of absence to complete the commission. County Hall was officially opened in 1963 by Prince Phillip.

In 1966, after 33 years of underground mining, Norman left the pits and took the risk of becoming a professional artist, little knowing how successful he was to become. Norman Cornish belongs to a generation of men who were denied the right of universal secondary education. Many men, and indeed women, of that era were forced by the financial hardships of the times to seek employment merely to sustain their families. This was not seen as altruism but as a duty. Perhaps despite, but probably because of this, Norman observes the human condition through very humane and compassionate eyes. His characters are all drawn

Robert Heslop - Domino Players, Silkscreen Print, 1940s

from life, not posed. They never show malice nor even disaffection. The characters he draws reflect the life they have lived. Their faces and figures map their experience. Norman often reflects on the time he spent at the Settlement – a time he sees as his 'university education' - attending what he considers to be Bill Farrell's *'university of life'*.

The work of Bob Heslop and Norman Cornish was subjected to close scrutiny and comparison in the 1940 Settlement exhibition by the London art organiser and professional artist G. Stevens. He likens Norman's sketch of a young girl reading, entitled 'Dreams', to the work of Rossetti but it is the oil painting of a mining scene entitled 'Dust' that occasions most comment when juxtaposed with Bob Heslop's highly detailed 'Coal Cutter and Conveyor'. The two works are described as striking, being examples of two contrasting schools of art – the Impressionist and the Realist. Paradoxically, Stevens refers to Norman's 'impressionistic' painting as the more realistic of the two works

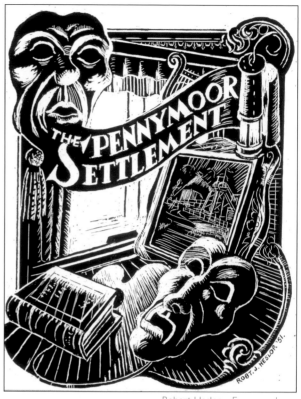

Robert Heslop - Everyman Logo
(Photo courtesy of The Spennymoor Settlement)

conveying as it does the effect of the dust and grime of the mine. "The artist has used low toned colours and the figures of the men working the skip hoist is very confused hid by the ever-present dust. On the other hand Mr Heslop has specialised in detail and the operator of a similar machine in his painting stands out prominently," Stevens commented. The two men were to be the joint contributors to a work entitled 'The Domino Players', a screen print that was based on an original design by Norman Cornish and printed by Bob Heslop. Bob had studied the art of screen printing whilst spending some time in London under the tutelage of Francis and Dorothy Carr, instructors at the Guildford School of Art. Bob had an innate sense of design which he used to good effect in his posters, greeting cards and scraperboard work. On the suggestion of Settlement member, Arnold Hadwin, he created the original classic motif for the 'Everyman Players' programmes ,depicting the masks of tragedy and comedy which reflected the Tisa Hess sculpture on the outside of the Theatre.

In a BBC Forces radio programme in January 1943 Bob Heslop stated, "The old beer and whippets miner is a thing of the past, the miner today is trying hard to make a worthy place for himself in the life of the country with interests in social affairs, painting, drama and music in his choirs and brass bands." Bob was to widen his own horizons quite literally when, in 1954, he was one of three miners in a delegation of eight industrial workers to be invited to visit Russia. Whilst there he continued to sketch but produced only one oil painting. The men were allowed down the mines and visited other industries but the expedition was described as a 'controlled' visit and was meticulously recorded in Bob's personal diaries.

Referring to the 1944 Settlement exhibition, the Auckland Chronicle of 27th July commented, "One always tends to group Mr Heslop and Mr Dees together…as primarily landscape painters…But this year both have made successful departures and by doing so have stressed their individualities – Mr Heslop with 'Mining Study', 'Pit Heap' and 'Coal Hewers' and Mr Dees with 'The Shows' and 'Corner End Study'…Mr Heslop sees life in the mine with a steady and unromantic eye and there is a savage tendency in his pictures of miners at work especially in 'Coal Hewers' where he breaks through the roof of a working and shows from above a group of miners at work. His 'Pit Heap' is definitely not a picture to enjoy in the ordinary sense of that word for there is an air of over-powering gloom in the great rearing mass of waste he has depicted with the trudging, work-bound men in its shadow."

chapter nine

Miner and child

Tom McGuinness - Miner & Child, Conté crayon, 1948

"I find it difficult to express myself in words. That's why I paint. I put my feelings into my paintings and my art mirrors my life in the mining community."

Tom McGuinness

Following the war years, Bill Farrell's Annual Reports document the Sketching Club's changing membership. The stalwarts, Bert Dees, Bob Heslop and the young Norman Cornish were joined at varying times by Jean Inglis, a young teacher (who in 1946 exhibited several mining scenes in

Jean Inglis - Portrait, Polymer

tempera). Bill Farrell commented , "[Jean was] much too young to have been caught up in the awful academic ways of most of her kind, she still paints because she wants to paint and joined us because we did not ask her to teach anybody else." Other members were Jack Roach, a blacksmith at Bearpark Colliery, Tom Alderson who was to become an art teacher, Arthur Bulman about whom no information is available and, in 1948, Tom McGuinness, the other famous mining artist from the Great Northern Coalfield to be associated with the Spennymoor Settlement, who is mentioned shortly after his perceptive and deeply moving conté drawing 'Miner and Child' had been bought by the Shipley Art Gallery in Gateshead.

Tom's pictorial record of the coal-mining industry will always remain unrivalled. He worked for thirty-nine years in the mines, painting daily what then seemed an indestructible industry. In his latter years he was to graphically illustrate the social consequences of the aftermath of the demise of the coal industry. Tom was a quiet, unassuming and gentle person with a keen interest in his fellow man. Whilst his subject matter epitomises and is firmly rooted in social realism, the depth of the emotion revealed raises Tom's work far above that of the documentary or the mere vernacular and places him in the forefront of contemporary expressionism.

Tom was born in Witton Park on 26th April 1926, the year of the General Strike, in a village that had been both a product and a victim of the Industrial Revolution. Witton Park's disused engine houses, broken railway lines and derelict pit-headgear stimulated his imagination and his emerging observational faculties which would become one of the fundamental skills that would underpin Tom's paintings. The background of poverty and protracted unemployment, together with his strong Catholic faith, undoubtedly influenced his views on life and reinforced his sense of social justice and community which is manifest in his personal diary - his art. Leaving school at fourteen Tom had several short-term jobs until he was introduced to his life-long passion, the coal industry, by sheer chance when he was conscripted to the coal mines in 1944 as a Bevin Boy. Despite the offer of employment as a professional artist, Tom was to spend the next thirty nine years working in the mine - the main source of his artistic inspiration.

During the war, he attended art classes in Darlington before joining the Spennymoor Settlement. It was Bill Farrell who persuaded Tom to draw from life and it was here, through discussions with other artists, especially Norman Cornish, that he began to experiment with different media and his

Tom McGuinness - Early Morning Shift, Oil, 1959 (Courtesy of MIMA, Middlesbrough)

characteristic style was to emerge. Tom was always keen to master new techniques and to adapt his style. His early images are in pencil, ink, pastel or conté crayon. By the early 1950s, during his time at the Spennymoor Settlement, he moved to oil painting and began to evolve the characteristic McGuinness style. By the early 1960s he had refined his technique to master the use of glazes which give his oil paintings an inner luminescence, a quality also apparent in his later stained-glass windows. He went on to develop his 'wash-off' technique, using layers of gouache and indian ink to produce powerful mining images. Tom, a superb printmaker, began etching in the early 1970s and in 1976 was awarded a Northern Arts Print Bursary to study lithography. Tom's prints, numbering over 100, made his work affordable and accessible to a new clientele - his work colleagues.

Tom McGuinness - Back Shift, Watercolour, 1983

Tom distorts all elements of the image - colour, line, tone and composition - using this legitimate artistic device to add emphasis, power and emotion to the picture. His paintings reveal the intangible. Much beauty and meaning can be revealed in the tragic and so Tom's miners become universal symbols of the suffering of man. His iconography includes powerful religious, political and social statements giving greater meaning than the image might initially imply.

Tom's remarkable body of work documents an industry that has been consigned to history. His images are a personal record of the miner's life. Painting as a true artist, for himself, Tom sees the world in a distortion of reality; his work colleagues are bent, almost cowed, by their awesome task. Their twilight subterranean world is illuminated by an eerie, ethereal light. His desire to chronicle the miner's lot has inspired a working pitman to produce the best, most accurate and complete artistic record of any industry. Tom was a quiet man who spoke powerfully through his art.

John (Jack) Joseph Roach [1911 – 1989] was born in Trimdon Village and left school to serve his time as a blacksmith, spending most of his working life at Bearpark Colliery until, after suffering a back injury in the 1950s, he retrained as a watch and clock maker at Finchale Training Centre for the Disabled. A self-taught artist who originally used watercolours, Jack, on completing a two year correspondence course in which he received critical appreciation of his work from Sam Spencer RA from Keighley, began to embrace other techniques. He joined the Spennymoor Settlement Sketching Club in 1945. Mainly interested in landscape painting, Jack's son John says that his father was encouraged to paint mining scenes by Sid Chaplin who realised that the embryonic National Coal Board was actively collecting mining pictures. Jack reluctantly painted the pits and indeed many of his mining scenes are essentially landscapes in which there happens to be a coalmine. He exhibited both locally and nationally and his work was included in exhibitions in both the Shipley and Laing Art Galleries on Tyneside and in the 1947 NCB 'Art by the Miner' exhibition which was launched in London before touring nationally. It was said of him in the catalogue accompanying the Artists' International Association exhibition 'The Coalminers' in 1950, "Roach is a blacksmith by trade an artist by nature. He has a passion for colour. Draughtsmanship is a mere framework on which he can exercise his paint which he uses lavishly, modelling the forms with his brush. Out of the Durham scene, he takes each object, distils it to its essential pigment and builds these into a mosaic." His trademark is his bold free style with paint applied thickly in an impasto of vivid colour. He took naturally to oil painting and all his later work was in this medium.

Professional artist and art teacher Tom Alderson, born in 1920, came from a mining family from Coundon, near Bishop Auckland. Contrary to the accepted local practice Tom's father, who was a miner in Westerton, was determined that his son would not follow him down the mine. After his war service with the RAF Tom became increasingly interested in art and design, He had heard of the Spennymoor Settlement and went to see one of its exhibitions in the late 1940s where he was introduced to Warden Bill Farrell. He enjoyed the camaraderie of the Sketching Club and the informal discussions in Norman Cornish's house after the meetings. To advance his career Bill Farrell advised Tom to enrol for formal art classes at Darlington School of Art where he won a scholarship to study fine art and graphic design at the London Central School of Art. Tom exhibited work in Settlement exhibitions. His interest, however, lay in the natural world, still life and abstraction. Although he returned to live in Coundon he has never drawn inspiration from his mining roots.

In 1949 Sketching Club members were to exhibit at the Artists' International Association exhibition in London. This Association had been founded in the 1930s as an anti-Fascist movement and its members consisted of such prominent names as Clive and Vanessa Bell, Duncan Grant, Julian Trevelyan, Stepehen Spender, Henry Moore and Mischa Black. In 1936 the Spennymoor Settlement members had made the acquaintance of the young German countess Elisabeth von der Schulenberg, known familiarly as Tisa Hess [1903 – 2001]. Tisa, the daughter of a German general, had married Jewish businessman Fritz Hess

Tom McGuinness - Night Shift, Aquatint Etching, 1977

and they had been encouraged to leave Germany in 1934 because of the rise of the Nazi regime. Unlike the rest of their family she and her brother Fritz held strong anti-Nazi views. Her brother was later to be executed for his part in the failed assassination attempt on Hitler's life by the Stauffenberg Group. Tisa, unusually for a noblewoman at the time, had studied art at the Berlin Academy of Art in the 1920s and had become friends with some of the leading intellectuals, including Bertholdt Brecht, Erich Remarque and Oskar Kokoschka.

Jack Roach - Bearpark Colliery, Oil, c1950s

On arriving in London with her husband, Tisa states in her autobiography 'Sketches from Life' that they both wanted to become English and tried to fit in. They were befriended by the architect Ernst Freud, the son of Siegmund and father of Lucian and himself a German émigré, who introduced them to his circle of friends. These included professional people and artists. In 1935 Tisa and her husband moved to a weekend cottage, built for them by Ernst, in Walberswick, a small village on the East Anglian coast where a number of artists and writers lived. She had a small studio which had previously been rented to Henry Moore to whom she was introduced by the artist John Skeaping.

Henry Moore showed an interest in her work and offered constructive criticism which made Tisa realise the limitations of her own ability to produce truly three dimensional forms and that her forte was in the two dimensional image. "…Seeing Henry Moore's work I understood the nature of sculpture. I was fascinated. Is there a moment for every artist when he must acknowledge his limitations? This encounter with Henry Moore meant just that for me. I couldn't get 'round' a sculpture. They remained reliefs. Reliefs, or rather drawings in wood or stone or bronze were my speciality." It was via this connection with Henry Moore that Tisa was to become involved with the anti-fascist Artists' International Association.

Tisa herself recalled, "In the summer of 1936 as a result of a chance meeting with an elderly lady whilst staying at Walberswick I learned of the 'distressed areas' of Britain and in particular the North East and was invited to visit the County Durham coalfield to give a lecture about art in the workers clubs and to give wood carving demonstrations… In 1937 I went there again, I was invited to visit a settlement in Spennymoor, a small mining town. The miners, whether they were in employment or not, had only one subject of conversation: their pit. This world down below held them in its spell."

Tom Alderson - Denise, Oil, 1950

Tisa was to spend a profitable time teaching the Settlement members drawing and carving in wood and hers was the only direct tuition the Sketching Club members were to receive. Settlement member Jack Green was skilled in working with wood and contributed to the dramatic activities of the Settlement as a stage and scenery carpenter and was a willing pupil of Tisa's. The Northern Echo in an article of 9th December 1937 commented, "Jack Green has profited from his contacts with Miss Hess for he has carved a powerful little mask cut in oak, together with other articles that have been turned on a lathe with his usual careful craftsmanship." He went on to exhibit woodcarvings at the Laing Art Gallery, Newcastle in 1940, 1941 and 1947. Norman Cornish assisted Jack with the designs for some of his carvings.

Tisa went on to exhibit three large pencil drawings of Durham miners, studies for future sculptures, in the 1937 Settlement exhibition and has left a permanent legacy in the sandstone carving of the masks of comedy and tragedy which adorn the outside of the Spennymoor Settlement. Dick Beavis, a Settlement member at the time, in his publication 'What Price Happiness?' recalls, "… At that time the settlement was still in the throes of being modernised and Tisa wanted to carve a headstone to be placed on the top of the building; two heads bonded together denoting worker and teacher united. Trevor Buckley, who had such a rugged head, was chosen as the worker … I do not know who sat for the woman's face, but the stone is still there all weathered away now. It depicts what the Settlement stood for – Worker and Teacher bonded together means progress." (Trevor Buckley had been wounded whilst serving in the International Brigade fighting the fascists in the Spanish Civil War. He was one of the jobless and by his own confession had always been in trouble with the police. With a passionate love of freedom he tramped miles to political meetings whilst Tisa Hess recalled his quiet humour and friendliness).

The carving remained in situ until May 2000 when it was removed to prevent further deterioration as it had been badly damaged by the elements. A copy was installed in its place and the original awaits funds to ensure its full restoration. When the stone was removed hidden papers were discovered in an envelope behind the sculpture and were sent for analysis. Sadly they disintegrated before they could be documented. Tisa herself made no reference to this hidden archive in her autobiography.

Tisa Hess - The Spennymoor Letter, Lithograph, 1970s

Following a retrospective exhibition of Tisa's work at Bishop Auckland Town Hall in June 2001, Settlement member Arnold Hadwin who went on to become editor of The Evening Despatch, wrote in the Northern Echo of the 18th June, "She had given up her class, her parents, her country and was desperately trying to find something to replace them. She still read the Bible avidly. But it was in Spennymoor that she realised an artist had to live with the working classes to be anything more than a dilettante." Arnold Hadwin went on, "Long ago, I recorded her words: 'I remember standing in front of thirty men in caps and mufflers, faces thin and emaciated. I was struck dumb. But I stayed on to teach them how to carve. It was in Spennymoor that the door to England slowly opened. I had found a community I could serve; a cause that inspired me. The men in their poverty were carefree and easy-going. I heard them laugh more than grumble. An indomitable love of freedom, irresistible and sometimes unaccountable gentleness (yes, even shyness) – these were for me the typical qualities I had been looking for for so long'."

Tisa's experiences in Spennymoor and the plight of the unemployed there gave her a lifelong concern for distressed and repressed peoples which was to be continually reflected in her art. This deep concern can be demonstrated by an incident recounted by Arnold. Whilst Tisa was

Jack Green - Newspaper Boy, Wood Carving, 1940s

interpreting for displaced female refugees in Hamburg after the war the occupying forces provided hundreds of pairs of wooden clogs, crude and ugly. She scrounged tins of red, yellow and green paint so that the women could have something colourful on their feet, commenting that that gave the women some dignity. She was to be so profoundly moved by the revelations of the Holocaust that she renounced the world and, in 1948, entered a convent in Dorsten and became known as Sister Paula.

Whilst remaining in the convent as a teaching nun Tisa continued to pursue her obsession with her art and, in the 1970s, shortly before fulfilling a lifelong ambition to return to her beloved North

The Spennymoor Settlement

Tisa Hess at Jarrow Slake, 1970s (Photo courtesy of The Guardian)

East of England where her work was to be exhibited both at Middlesbrough and The Bede Gallery, Jarrow, she executed a series of thirteen lithographs known as the Spennymoor Letter. These were dedicated to the suffering of the Durham miners in the 1930s and were her own pictorial diary of the men and the conditions she found there and which continued to haunt her. She never forgot the poverty she had witnessed in Spennymoor and at all times carried a little bag, containing a crust of bread, on a string around her neck, to symbolise that she would never starve. She died in the convent on 8th February 2001 aged 97.

The Sketching Club was to continue even after the Spennymoor Settlement had ceased to exist in its original form. Bill and Betty Farrell left in 1954 when funding was withdrawn. No new permanent members were to join after 1952 but the Club continued to meet each Saturday afternoon as usual as Norman Cornish assured the Farrells in a letter inviting them to his May/June 1960 exhibition at the Stone Gallery, Newcastle. He went on to say "… but I do not attend very regularly I'm afraid because there is so much work to be done at home… Bert Dees, John (Bob) Heslop and Jack Roach are all in good health and spirits. You are still there, in every part of it, and it shall always be so."

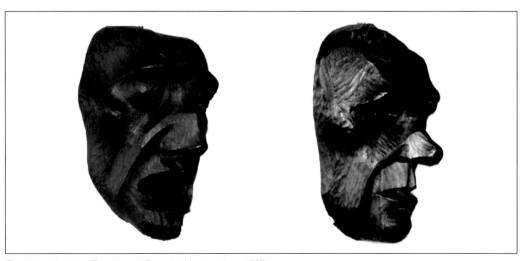

Tisa Hess - Masks of Tragedy and Comedy, Woodcarving, c1937

chapter ten

Learning and literature

Jack Maddison with Bill & Betty Farrell

Where runs this weary road?
To what distant point in darkness do you run?

Where ends these gleaming rails?
And rings that signal bell in some eternal hell?

Where sucks that gaping pipe?
What bitter waters flow?
Only a miner may know.

Sid Chaplin 'The Miner Knows'

The Theatre Group and the Sketching Club were the two most consistently successful strands of the Settlement's educational programme. Many of the other classes and courses were more transient, reflecting demand and the availability of provision. Even so it became apparent at an early stage that Bill and Betty Farrell required additional professional help to fulfil the demand, hence Jack Maddison was appointed as Sub-Warden on 1st February 1933 and, together with his wife Mary, moved to live above the joinery shop in King Street, Spennymoor. Jack was originally a pitman from Coundon. He went to Ruskin College, Oxford and was an honours graduate in Economics and Political Theory. Jack completed his teacher training at Alnwick where he was to become friendly with the Trevelyan family from Wallington Hall, Northumberland. His academic background and inspirational teaching-style proved a huge asset to the Settlement's development as an educational centre. While teaching maths in a school at Boldon Colliery he used the analogy of betting on horses to engage the pupils' attention and even created an electrical system which he used to demonstrate mathematical principles in a practical way.

Jack Maddison & Children at Play (Photo courtesy of Rene Chaplin)

Jack taught and encouraged many Settlement members to further their education and held outreach classes in history and economics at Coundon and other outlying villages. It was these classes that Mary Cooke from Leasingthorne attended who, after leaving school, had spent seven years in domestic service at Newton Cap and went on to study social work at Bishop Creighton House, Fulham, one of the London settlements. She was to win the Mary Macather Scholarship which allowed her to go to Geneva for special training in economics and social science. Even so she spent a lot of time at the Spennymoor Settlement during vacations. Tom Vickerstaff, a coal hewer at Dean and Chapter Colliery for sixteen years, travelled to Spennymoor Settlement several days each week to study under Jack Maddison. He went on to Fircroft College, Birmingham to study history, economics, literature and philosophy. Yet another of Jack's students, Thomas Pinch of Stillington, Stockton was awarded a scholarship from Avoncroft College, Worcestershire to study agricultural sciences, history and economics. In all some twenty eight members of the Spennymoor Settlement went on to colleges of higher education including Arnold Hadwin – later editor of The Northern Despatch – who went to Oriel College, Oxford, a great achievement for someone from the working classes. Arnold acknowledges the great debt he owes to Jack Maddison's inspirational teaching and commonsense approach to activities at the Settlement. It was Jack who would canvass for members in the working men's clubs and despite his high socialist ideals, his feet remained firmly on the ground. He was to stay at the Settlement for fifteen years until the funding difficulties of 1947 forced him to leave.

Sid Chaplin (1916 – 1986), originally a miner at Dean and Chapter Colliery, Ferryhill, was to become one of the North East's most prominent writers and a great influence on many of the new wave of 'working class writers' of the 1950s and 1960s such as Keith Waterhouse, Alan Sillitoe, Stan Barstow, Alan Plater and John Braine. Sid was born at 23 Bolckow Street, Shildon. On leaving school at the age of fourteen he originally trained as a barber but soon followed his father into the coal industry working as a blacksmith at Dean and Chapter Colliery, Ferryhill, where his father was a colliery electrician. An avid reader from an early age with a tremendous thirst for knowledge, Sid was attracted to the Spennymoor Settlement when he heard there was a lending library there on Mondays and Thursdays. His widow, Rene, tells us that "He literally got on his bike and went to see it."

Norman Cornish - Sid Chaplin, Oil

In the Spennymoor Settlement's 21st Birthday Commemorative Magazine Sid remembers in his feature 'The Bicycle Against the Wall', "It all started with an old bicycle I bought for thirty bob. Otherwise I would probably have continued to take the shortest road out of Spennymoor for a few years longer. But I bought that old bicycle, and it wasn't bad for an old bone shaker, so I started making detours. One of those detours led me along King Street one day, and I saw some people coming out of a building with books under their arms. I hadn't much idea of what the Settlement was, but I was book-hungry, tired of westerns and adventures, so I propped my bicycle against the wall and went in. …It was love at first sight and before long the handlebars of my bike spent long hours conversing with the walls and those wide windows while I browsed among good books and good pictures and made some good friends … and so the Settlement became my university, opening out new horizons and providing me with a good stout staff to take me towards them."

Being the oldest of six children Sid had always been a natural storyteller, making up stories for his younger siblings and he had always been interested in writing, penning letters to The Northern Echo signed 'Young Vigilante' or 'Vance 111'. Bill Farrell encouraged Sid to write. In a letter dated the 18th September 1938 regarding the type-script of a play, Bill gives constructive criticism and ends "… I think it is a grand effort … you must carry on with this you have made the first very difficult beginning." However, it was Jack Maddison, the Sub-Warden of the Settlement and a lifelong friend, who convinced Sid he should apply for a scholarship to Fircroft Working Men's College, Birmingham. Sid had studied political theory and economics with Jack and, despite intending to study economics at college, he and his tutors agreed that his potential lay in the world of literature. Sid's son Michael tells us, "When he went to Fircroft he was soon removed from the economics class and sent to do literature. The tutor said his economics were inexact but jolly interesting!" The outbreak of war put paid to Sid's college ambitions, however, and he returned to Durham and the mines working as a belt fitter but knowing that his future lay in writing.

Sid married Rene on 1st January 1941 and went on to have three children, Chris, Gillian and Michael who was to become a scriptwriter for television and theatre. In 1946, whilst living in 9, Gladstone Terrace, Ferryhill, Sid published his first collection of short stories 'The Leaping Lad' which won him the Atlantic Award for Literature. Set in the mining villages of County Durham, this

Norman Cornish - Dean & Chapter Colliery, Pastel

work established him as an interpreter of pit life and drew comparisons with D.H. Lawrence. The £300 prize money allowed him to take time away from the colliery to complete his first novel, 'My Fate Cries Out', featuring the lead miners of Weardale. He honed his writing skills by contributing articles to the NCB's 'Coal News' and eventually became their feature writer, travelling extensively throughout the coalfields.

Sid's novel, 'The Thin Seam', set in the Durham Coalfield, which featured five wash drawings by the Yorkshire mining artist Norman Town, was to become the inspiration for the moving musical play 'Close the Coalhouse Door', a collaboration between Sid and Alan Plater with music by Alex Glasgow. During the 1950s and 60s Sid went on to produce a steady stream of publications, the

Norman Cornish - A Bit Crack, Flomaster Pen

most notable being 'The Day of the Sardine', the story of a working class lad growing up in a Northern industrial environment. He contributed to the BBC television series 'When the Boat Comes In' and was a regular feature writer for the Guardian newspaper. In October 1971 Sid finally devoted himself to full time writing publishing 'The Smell of Sunday Dinner' a compilation of various newspaper articles.

He continued to produce books with a Northern flavour and his contribution to regional culture was recognised when he was awarded a Master of Arts Degree by Newcastle University and an Honorary Fellowship by Sunderland Polytechnic. Sid's national status was confirmed with the award of the OBE. The legacy of Sid Chaplin continues, not only as the inspiration for a new generation of writers of working-class fiction, but as the catalyst for the writing of short stories via the annual Sid Chaplin Short Story Competition, organised by the town council of his home town of Shildon.

Arnold Hadwin, successful journalist and newspaper editor, was to have contact with the Spennymoor Settlement for twenty years, beginning when he joined the Children's Section as a four year old in 1934. He went on to join the Settlement Scout Group. The youngest of eight he came from a working class background with his father working as a fitter and turner at the Weardale Iron and Coal Company. Arnold freely admits that he would not have become a professional journalist had it not been for his contact with the Settlement. Educated at the Alderman Wraith Secondary School, Spennymoor, National Service saw Arnold in the Marine Commandos which had stringent entry criteria. His natural physical fitness which had been

British Troops leaving Israel in 1948. (Arnold Hadwin 3rd from right)

honed by his appetite for cross-country running made him an ideal candidate for the Marines. By the age of nineteen, in 1948, he was reporting happenings in Palestine and Haifa and was responsible for compiling incidents and weekly intelligence reports which were circulated to his commanding officer.

Arnold continued his association with the Settlement on his return from active service and even, together with Edna, his future wife, took part in Bill Farrell's 1951 production of Strindberg's 'Easter'. None of Arnold's siblings went into higher education or academia whilst Arnold, after having attended Jack Maddison's economics class, was persuaded to undertake higher education, initially at Ruskin College, Oxford. There, after two years, he obtained a Diploma in Politics, Philosophy and Economics and was encouraged to apply to Oriel College and in his words "never looked back."

After graduation he became industrial correspondent for the Guardian newspaper and went on to become editor of the Evening Despatch in 1964 before moving on to the editorship of the Bradford Telegraph and Argus in 1973. Despite not living in the North East for many years, Arnold's continuing gratitude and support for the Settlement can be deduced from his attendance at Settlement events. Both Sid Chaplin and Arnold Hadwin acknowledged the encouragement, guidance and mentorship they received from Jack Maddison who was described as an inspirational and innovative teacher and to quote Rene Chaplin "the nicest man I knew."

The literary legacy of the Settlement continued into the new millennium with best-selling novelist Wendy Robertson who used the Settlement as inspiration for her 2001 novel, 'Where Hope Lives'. "The characters and events of the novel are entirely and absolutely fictional," states Wendy, "however, in writing it, I was inspired by the work of the Settlement movement and its objective as the provision of a meeting place where people could experience the intellectual stimulation of wide discussion, the practice of arts and crafts and access to artists of national reputation." Wendy paid particular tribute to the writings of Sid Chaplin and the work of painters Tisa Hess, Norman Cornish and Tom McGuinness whose iconic 'Miner and Child' was reproduced as a frontispiece for the novel. "Looking and looking and looking at their work has been, for me, the most pleasurable part of the research for this novel," proclaimed Wendy.

chapter eleven

Means Test to majesty

Caravan City, Spennymoor 1930s (Photo courtesy of Durham University Library)

"The stark tragedy is that so early in life they [the unemployed] have changed from being men with a future to being men with a past…
There but for the Settlement, walk I."

Harry Vickerstaff

The work of the Settlement was not confined to the education of the working class and the socially disadvantaged. Bill Farrell drew upon his knowledge of the social sciences to study the psychological effects of unemployment and social deprivation. In 1932 – 1933 in his annual report he wrote that there were three identifiable emotional levels associated with unemployment. These he defined as an initial halcyon period during the first nine months when the novelty of not working seemed like a prolonged holiday – this group was not looking for help and was not attracted to the Settlement; the second period when unemployment benefit ceased, savings were exhausted and there was an inability to maintain even a subsistence standard of living, the unemployed began to feel isolated and humiliated by the Means Test – this group was angry and willing to accept help from the Settlement for self betterment; and finally, after two years of idleness, the unemployed became apathetic, ceased to struggle, no longer cared and became incapable of self-help. There was a total loss of pride and they were prepared to accept any form of charity. These men were beyond redemption from the Settlement. The practical significance of this observation was the ability to identify the critical periods in an unemployed man's life when he would both be open to and capable of receiving the kind of educational help that the Settlement could offer.

The Social Service Group of Settlement members continued these pioneering sociological studies by undertaking an authoritative and analytical survey into 'The Budgets of the Unemployed'. "As the budget to be discussed was that of a family, the first point to be decided was that of the composition of the family unit. This was eventually agreed upon as a man, wife

Tom McGuinness - Pigeon Crees, Oil, 1953

Norman Cornish - The Allotment Men, Mixed Media

and three children of five, nine and twelve years. The income of this family was based upon the allowances of the Unemployment Assistance Board and this was taken to be 37s. 6d ... The curve of food consumption is one that shoots quickly up to its maximum on pay day and thereafter declines more or less sharply until the day before pay day when it is at its minimum. This means that there are certain days when food is scarce. The general diet is monotonous broken only by articles like currants. When money has to be found for emergencies, these articles are regarded as luxuries and dispensed with. This makes a monotonous diet even more monotonous. In any case, it is a question of saving pennies only but these are very important. Indeed, it is the penny that is the real legal tender of the unemployed... Only by very good management on the part of the woman is existence possible. There is no thought of the future because they are utterly unable to project themselves out of the present. They know no peace. Neither can they be said to have a life..." J. Newsom stated in his book 'Out of the Pit.' The subsequent report and its conclusions were later raised in Parliament by Hugh Dalton, Member of Parliament for Bishop Auckland, to reinforce the socialist view that the distribution of benefits should be centralised to ensure uniformity of financial provision for the unemployed nationwide.

In 1938 this group undertook a further piece of research – an enquiry into how the people of Spennymoor spent their leisure hours contrasted with how they'd like to spend them. The wife of an unemployed miner, Mrs Richard Vickerstaff from Kirk Merrington, remarking that the attitude of the Durham miner towards his wife had changed a good deal, said, "Instead of looking upon her as a drudge he is willing to help as much as he can and let her have as much freedom as possible. That is the reason a large number of women take an active part in social life and make more use of their leisure time than do the men ... The problem of a girl leaving school is solved in most cases by sending her away into domestic service, regardless of the fact that a lot of the girls would like to be trained for a profession, such as nursing. It has always been the custom for the mother to train the girl and she naturally expects her to take up her own life at 14 or 15 years.

In the case of boys however, it has always been different, work having always been found for them at the local pits. That is why we find today the objection to boys leaving home. Boys in our district have never been trained to look after themselves, the family having the idea that a boy, having done his day's work, it was nothing but right that he should be attended to."

The pioneering work of the Settlement was recognised nationally when, on 6th December 1934, the then Prince of Wales, whilst on a tour of the depressed areas, visited the Spennymoor Settlement. The Prince was no stranger to the North East having visited some six years previously when he was seen as a supporter and sympathiser in the working man's struggle to overcome the evils of unemployment and economic depression. James R. Spencer reporting the visit in his Sunday Sun article stated, "No one could know the Prince more intimately than the Durham miner.

Norman Cornish - Group of boys out walking

He has spoken to HRH by his own cottage fireside, he has stood with him in the black mud of his pit village street, he has shown him his handiwork in many kinds of productive labour other than coalmining. And, as in the war days, the soldiers fighting in Flanders' bloody trenches, appreciated having the King's eldest son to stand by them in their danger, so the Durham miners welcome him today … in the hour of their direst domestic danger. For it is more than loyalty which

Norman Cornish - Study of heads

makes the miner and his wife open their homes and hearts to the Prince of Wales. In him they see more than a Royal sympathiser. They see him as a Royal helpmate … above all else the Prince has shown the north that he is a man of action."

On arrival the Prince was given a great reception and the strong police presence had difficulty in controlling the crowd who were eager to greet the royal visitor. His Highness was met by Bill and Betty Farrell, the Sub-Warden Jack Maddison, Ann Hodgson, Chairman of the Members' Association, Councillor A. Blenkin, Chairman of Spennymoor Urban District Council and Mr C. F. Meikle, Clerk to the Council. As the Prince moved between the sections of needlework, carpentry and boot repairing the Settlement Scouts provided a guard of honour. He was impressed by the various schemes and cultural activities which were being undertaken in the Settlement and he was astonished to learn that the paintings on display were the work of the members themselves. Each one was original. Not one was a copy. For landscapes the men had gone out into the local countryside, for portraits they had taken local residents as models. The media widely reported this visit, commenting that a school of art, or a 'Pitman's Academy' (when the name was first coined) founded by ex-miners, was not outside the bounds of probability.

The Spennymoor Settlement

Scout Guard of Honour for Prince of Wales visit, March 1934
(L to R - Bill Farrell, Prince of Wales, Jack Maddison and Betty Farrell)

From the inception of the concept of a settlement at Spennymoor there had been the intention of forging links with the local university as at Toynbee Hall in London. In his original report to Toynbee Hall Bill Farrell had noted that the local university, Durham, did not have a School of Social Science on site. In fact the nearest faculty of Social Science was situated in Newcastle and although at that time technically a college of Durham University, the physical location some thirty miles north of Spennymoor and the fact that it was administered by another county, made liaison impractical. Almost immediately after his arrival in Spennymoor, therefore, Bill Farrell identified the Church colleges in Durham as a potential source of co-operation, realising that religious students needed more than a working knowledge of the Social and Behavioural Sciences. He pursued this idea in a long series of correspondence with the Rev Dr E.G. Pace, Master of Hatfield College, Durham.

Whilst Bill Farrell's vision and long term objective seemed to have been the creation of a Workers' University with faculties of Mining Sciences, and Social and Behavioural Sciences, the correspondence led to a seemingly more practical alternative – the creation of a daughter settlement, affiliated to and administered by Durham University and being located in university property. The embryo settlement, Durham House, which came into existence in July 1933, was to have similar aims to the Spennymoor Settlement and ultimately a joint administration committee was formed to co-ordinate the functions of not only these two settlements but also to include a new settlement located at Seaham. Financial constraints after the Second World War meant that effectively the Spennymoor Settlement was administered from Durham.

chapter twelve
The last act

Cast of 'The Long Mirror' by J.B. Priestley, 1951

"unemployment could be a blessing if accepted and used in the correct way - the opportunity of leisure."

Ironically the end of war also signified the end of unemployment in Spennymoor. Bill Farrell, in common with many other observers of the time, questioned in his 1940 Annual Report, "To what will we return when hostilities cease? ...who can doubt that but for a time a greater lassitude will descend upon us while industrial, physical, mental and social unemployment and poverty will be more widespread then ever before?" This brief but poignant statement gives a vivid insight into the gravity of the desperation and despair that had accompanied the pre-war unemployment in Spennymoor. Bill Farrell is implying that he may rather be involved in a war with Germany, a war which, however, had brought full employment, than return to the dark days of pre-war misery.

Country Dance Festival, Brancepeth Castle, 1936 (Back Row L to R - ?, Mrs. Knaggs, Annie Rutherford, Beattie Rutter, Hannah Marley, Esther Pollock, Janet Brickley. Front Row L to R - ?, Mary Robinson, Margaret Spence, Joan Cornish (nee Robinson), Mary Grainger (nee Pollock)

Despite this apparent tone of despair the 1945 post-war syllabus new membership year, beginning on 1st October 1945, still offered a comprehensive programme which included a Junior Library, County Library, Women's Group, Male-Voice Choir, Junior Folk Dance, Elementary French and German, Girls' Mime and Dance, W.E.A. 'Modern Problems' Class, Wolf Cubs, Theatre Company, Boy Scouts and Sketching Club. Bill Farrell in collaboration with Arts Council for Great Britain (formerly the Council for the Encouragement of Music and the Arts - CEMA) continued to arrange concerts and exhibitions of paintings and other works of art in the theatre. The programme was "by no means complete nor is it unchangeable." Membership was open to all persons aged 14 or over at a charge of 4s per year, minors' subscription was 2s 6d per annum. Honorary membership was offered to all who sympathised with the aims and objectives of the Spennymoor Settlement but who were not able to enrol in any Class or Group, and from whom subscriptions were invited without any fixed and stated sum.

William Mason in his dissertation of 1954, however, commented, "…It is not without significance that all the old Settlement groups in Spennymoor, with the exception of the Theatre Company, have died off one by one during the past ten years. The death of the last group, the woodworkers, in 1951 is solemnly recorded in the twentieth annual report. 'It used to be one of our finest craft groups,' wrote the Warden, 'but the desire to do such work has faded with the increased economic prosperity. We found no new woodworker-artists, and the old ones do not practise the craft as much as heretofore.' The obituary notice of the Woodworkers' Group might also be read as applying to the Settlement as a whole. It must be concluded then that settlements are no longer needed in our society…The Spennymoor Settlement is the only one now remaining in Durham County. Durham House came to an end during the war; Bensham Grove Settlement, Gateshead is now a community centre; as is also Rock House Settlement, Seaham Harbour. The Spennymoor Settlement remains a settlement only in name, because that is provided for in the Trust deeds."

There was a perception in the 1950s that settlements were anachronistic in that they continued to offer educational opportunities which were increasingly better provided for elsewhere, particularly by the W.E.A. and the trend towards the Technical College. And indeed with post-war full employment the raison d'etre for Spennymoor Settlement had disappeared. Although still a time of austerity there was a relative increase in prosperity and a rise in optimism and expectation. The post- war working class expected more social and particularly recreational opportunities. As early as 1933 the Committee of the Member's Association at the Settlement, when asked to consider the following term's syllabus felt that, "The recreational side [of the Spennymoor Settlement] be now encouraged as the educational side had been tried but had not attracted many active members. We would suggest that the table tennis, draughts and chess be allowed to be played in the Common Room."

Although the Sunday Sun in 1951 referred to the Spennymoor Settlement as the 'Workers' University', the problems of finance were to end Bill Farrell's vision and ultimately his wardenship in 1954. Funding for the Spennymoor Settlement, originally via the Pilgrim Trust, became uncertain towards the end of the Second World War. War-time had seen reduced commitment amongst Settlement members whose time was increasingly taken up with the war effort. Nevertheless these years were to prove some of the most successful creatively with the Settlement hosting a major Festival of Art in 1942 which integrated all the Settlement's artistic endeavour into one cohesive whole. The War had brought full employment and a collective aim, nationally and regionally; ostensibly the main purpose for the Settlement's existence had been fulfilled. Even so, it had become an important social, educational and recreational asset to the town, an asset of which Spennymoor was justifiably proud and keen to continue to support. At the end of the War Bill Farrell stated, "It is pleasant to report that the Town now feels that the Settlement is its own permanent organisation and one of which the Town will go to some lengths to preserve. It is not so pleasant to record that it is still afraid that the Town itself cannot and apparently never will be able to pay for its keep."

The Pilgrim Trust continued to support the Settlement until April 1947 when the Trust accepted that the original social conditions that had required the funding of the Spennymoor Settlement were now past and that a 'Social Revolution' that levelled off the nation's income and introduced the National Insurance Act had taken place. Eventually, after protracted negotiations, Durham County Council became the major fund-holder, contributing two thirds of the Settlement's annual running costs of £2,000. In accordance with the recent Education Act of 1944, in order to receive the County's financial support, the Settlement had to adopt a new constitution and increase subscriptions (from four shillings to ten shillings and sixpence) in order to make good the shortfall, despite receiving £200 from the National Coal Board and a reported contribution of £335 from the L.E.A. together with support from Spennymoor Urban District Council.

Under the terms of the Settlement deeds, at their discretion the Trustees could, if the Settlement ceased to exist, sell the property and devote the money "to the benefit of the poor people of Spennymoor." They could also sanction the Settlement buildings' use in other ways which would seem likely to further the Settlement's original aims. In 1953, in order to try to safeguard the future of the Settlement with its proven educational track record, the Trustees proposed that Durham County Council collaborate with them to use the premises for the provision of Further Education, aspiring to become a major player in the County's educational strategy. Much discussion and correspondence took place but the proposal 'to collaborate' was rejected by Durham County Council in December 1953 and in a letter to the Trustees the authority appeared to misunderstand the debate and declined to 'acquire the premises'. Indeed in response to this letter Bill Farrell wrote on 30th December 1953, on behalf of the Trustees, giving notice to Durham County Council to cease using the premises as from 31st March 1954. Despite this notice to quit, the ever-optimistic Bill Farrell suggested to the Council that they should let him know if the Trustees had 'misconstrued' Durham County's original letter!

Bill Farrell, however, is on record, in a letter of 21st September 1953, as accepting that "unless a real change occurs within the next 6 months the Spennymoor Settlement WILL have to close down… But I am not in despair! Organisations come and go, but their work lives after them and nothing can undo the work the Spennymoor Settlement has done in the coalfield." Durham County Council's support ceased in April 1954. Although financial support from Spennymoor Urban District Council was still forthcoming, the withdrawal of funding from Durham County Council resulted in the Settlement becoming a voluntary organisation unable to afford a full-time Warden. "Why," asked the Auckland Chronicle of 4th February 1954, "when Durham County Council gives grants and large grants to community centres and youth clubs does it not make the maximum grant to this Settlement which has become something of a spear-head of cultural activity in the County?"

Spennymoor Settlement formally closed on 31st March 1954.

chapter thirteen

Exit – stage right

Tea on the lawn with Betty Farrell, Mina Martin and Bill Farrell (Photo courtesy of Rene Chaplin)

"Let us not think of tomorrow lest we disappointed be."

Tommy Armstrong

Bill Farrell had been approached on Thursday 18th March 1954 by members Molly Kane and Paula Armstrong to ask if he would have any objection to them organising a public petition to be sent to Durham County Council asking it to "reconsider its decision not to grant aid the Spennymoor Settlement." Bill's delight is obvious from his daily diary entry, " ...this day my heart leaped. Here was to be real action at last. The thing I have been waiting for, some sign that somebody amongst our members cared enough about us to get 'cracking' on the streets and from door to door. This is the only KIND of action which Durham County Councillors will understand: it is as POLITICAL as is their denial of us, and it will get some reaction. I blessed their enterprise but told them the Settlement as such and I as its Officer must not be entangled with it. Its virtue will lie in its utter lack of official inspiration and help. They are to form a small ACTION COMMITTEE on their own. EXCELLENT."

A last-ditch attempt by Bill Farrell, on Tuesday 30th March 1954, failed to convince the Trustees not to recommend a new, revised constitution which would replace the post of a paid Warden with that of a 'voluntary worker'. Bill contended that money could be raised on the surety of the Settlement buildings – sufficient to fund the running of the Settlement together with his continued salary. Being aware that the Warden of Toynbee Hall and fellow Trustee of Spennymoor Settlement, Jimmy Mallan, was secretly negotiating for funding for the Settlement behind the scenes with the Siemens Company in London, Bill tried to persuade his other Trustees to defer a decision on the revised constitution awaiting the outcome of those negotiations. Their plan was to discuss three possible options with the Siemens Board of Managing Directors in Woolwich. The first option was to ask for substantial grant-aid without any strings. The second option was again substantial grant-aid but with a local quid pro quo, giving special membership of the Settlement to the local factory employees in Spennymoor. The third option was for Bill Farrell to be taken into employment by Siemens as their local Welfare officer, to undertake special experimental work with their staff with the intention of

inducing their employees to use the Settlement's educational facilities. This latter option would have the effect of taking Bill Farrell off the Settlement payroll, but would allow him to remain as Warden. Bill felt this was a "good, sound scheme which would save the Settlement." Jim Mallan was to undertake a confidential approach at the London end. Fellow Trustees, Joe Elgey and Charles Meikle over-ruled Bill who records in his diary that they said, "we must act now, ACT in the light of the circumstances as they exist at this moment, cannot wait for Jimmy's report," thus recommending committing the Settlement to a future as a voluntary body without paid staff. A special meeting to 'consider and possibly adopt' the new, modified form of the 1948 constitution therefore was planned for Thursday 8th April.

Despite its uncertain future, activities at the Settlement had gone ahead as programmed. In his final Settlement diary Bill records that Bert Dees, Norman Cornish and himself painting together in the beech woods down the Old Page Bank line, Betty Wendel's Girl's Theatre School was growing in numbers, the Theatre

Children at Play - Folk Dancing

Company met to read Somerset Maugham's 'The Bread Winner', Bob Welch's Electrics Class, the Mime and Dance Class continued to meet on Thursdays and that Jean Grainger's Folk Dance Group party was attended by forty people. At this party Bill Farrell records, "I asked them not to think of this night as a FINAL night before a shut-down of the Settlement, assuring them that even if the Settlement, 'as at present constituted' ceased to be there would still be a Spennymoor Settlement." (Sadly the Folk Dancing Group was to end on Friday 14th May – after twenty three successful years).

By Thursday 1st April Molly Kane reported that 1800 townspeople had signed the petition as also had the Dean and Chapter Lodge of the Durham Miners' Association, whose signature carried the backing of another 2600 mine workers. Bill's delight was obvious, as his diary showed, "these signatures were got by some half dozen people in some six hours door to door canvass. Excellent, good i'faith. Molly, Betty Wendel, Hazel Wendel, Bob Welch, Bill Mason, John Hicks, Paula Armstrong and some of Betty Wendel's Girls' Club did the work. All honour to them."

Despite many well intentioned activities attempting to save the Settlement in its original form, the special meeting on Thursday 8th April was a disaster. Bill Farrell had successfully approached Billy Hirst, the Correspondence Secretary of the Dean and Chapter Colliery Lodge, who had agreed to intercede with Durham County Council's Education Committee on the Settlement's behalf. The clandestine negotiations with the Siemens Company could not be divulged at the meeting as this might prejudice future discussions. The Trustees had met previously to agree a plan to ask for an adjournment during this meeting as they felt the proposed new constitution must not go through in the light of these new initiatives to try to safeguard the future of the Settlement.

In his diary of 8th April Bill records "This meeting was the most dreadful I have ever attended. The malcontented splitting faction became vociferous, refused to accept the advice of the Officers to adjourn and shouted and argued with the Chairman, Mr Thurston who in the end left the chair. I then had to take charge of the meeting and wielded a big stick saying that 'this, the first time you are asked to act in a reasonable way as a responsible body you act like irresponsible children. I will now have to report that fact to the Trustees, whose trust and freedom you have now shown was misplaced.' The meeting broke up in some confusion with the two factions at loggerheads." The proposal to amend the constitution was carried by some thirty votes to twenty – a decision which condemned the Settlement to the status of a voluntary body without recourse to any funding. Bill Farrell's sense of isolation and rejection and his feelings of despondency and anger at the outcome of the meeting are manifest in his diary entry of the day "…I do now, indeed, feel ALONE …"

Previous histories have recorded that despite the continued funding from Spennymoor Urban Council it was the removal of funding by Durham County Council which led to the closure of the Settlement in its original form. However, the evidence from Bill Farrell's own diaries casts major doubt on the validity of that explanation. Of the meeting of Thursday 8th April Bill Farrell records, "Dean and Chapter Lodge's letter arrived at 3.30pm and too late to do anything about its contents before that night's meeting." Confusingly, whether or not the letter was read out to the meeting is not clear from the diary entry but as the advice to adjourn the meeting, pending further information and developments, was ignored, it does raise the possibility of the membership being ignorant of the letter's content.

Bill reveals in his diary entry of Friday 9th April that the letter from Dean and Chapter Lodge not only confirmed its support for the Settlement's cause by signing Molly Kane's petition but also confirmed that not only would they act as negotiator for the Settlement with Durham County

Council's Education Committee to discuss the Settlement's grants but that they actually, "HAD so met the Durham County Education Committee and had had an assurance from it that grants would be paid on certain conditions which, in effect, were those to which we had agreed and worked under up to two years ago. The leopard has NOT changed its spots, but there is some hope. BUT I must handle these delicate matters now as agreed upon yesterday and this fact, coupled with the fact that I could not give details of the Seimens' negotiations and had to withhold THAT gave rise to last night's dreadful meeting. I am now in an awful state and a dreadful predicament."

One wonders why the membership voted, as they did - effectively rejecting any grant - for an amended constitution and thus a voluntary organisation status, if the content of this letter had been divulged and fully understood. Could it have been that Bill Farrell's 'malcontents' saw this as an opportunity to oust him for what ever reason as Warden of the Spennymoor Settlement? There is evidence in Bill's own writings to suggest that he felt conspired against and isolated. In an attempt to reconcile this predicament a meeting was subsequently arranged for Monday 26th April at Shire Hall, Durham, the County Council headquarters between a delegation from the Settlement - George Bushel, Betty Wendel and Molly Kane – Dean and Chapter Lodge and the Education Committee. Ironically Bill Farrell was not present at this vital meeting as he had agreed, by accident or design, to attend an interview for a post in the new town of Stevenage! History does not contemporaneously record the outcome of this crucial meeting as even more curiously the pages of Bill Farrell's normally copious diaries are blank for the whole week beginning Saturday 24th April.

The Northern Echo of Thursday 13th May 1954 contained a report of the Durham County Council's Education Committee's meeting with delegates from the Settlement and Dean and Chapter Lodge and the receipt of the petition. The newspaper account stated that it was agreed that a public meeting would be called to discuss the Settlement's future. The delegates reported back to Bill Farrell that Durham County Council had agreed to grant aid the Settlement under certain terms and conditions. These would, in Bill Farrell's view, effectively mean the end of the Settlement per se with the proposed setting up of another body to run a community centre within the Settlement building. That body would have to raise £300 - £400 per annum as its share of the costs. Bill Farrell commented, "…I know it can not be done in Spennymoor. And now there is another overdraft mounting up and the repairs and cleaning work grows apace. No, it can not be done unless the STANDARDS of STAFF AND WORK as previously set are lowered to extinction." Bill Farrell penned a letter to the Director of Education asking for confirmation of the terms of the grant to enable a report to be given to the members. It would seem that whilst the County Council were prepared to make some gesture towards funding Bill Farrell felt this ran counter to the aims of the Settlement and was not acceptable.

The irony of this situation is that Bill Farrell was now effectively unemployed, with no income and at the age of 59 little prospect of employment – he was in the same position as the desperate men he had striven to help and to lead to a 'Way to the Better'.

chapter fourteen

The final curtain

Bill Farrell inspiring young artists (Photo courtesy of Rene Chaplin)

"He brought hope to a town of despair.
If a man should be remembered by his works –
and the works of the people he influenced –
Bill Farrell has an eternity in front of him."

Arnold Hadwin

The final months of Bill and Betty Farrell's occupancy of the Settlement were very difficult and disappointing especially when Bill's last hope of external funding disappeared when Siemens informed him on 1st July 1954 that they would not be offering financial assistance. A Special

General Meeting was called on 8th July of user members at which Bill Farrell told the thirty attendees, including fellow Trustees Charles Meilke and Joe Elgey, that the Settlement was bankrupt and there was only one course of action left to them – to sell the property. His advice was ignored and the members endorsed the previous decision of the 30th March and duly elected a new Chairman, Councillor George Thompson. The first meeting of the new committee took place two days later – Bill Farrell was not invited. A 'new Warden', one Harry Smith, had been elected and the Committee demanded that Bill Farrell provide an inventory and that he hand over all documents and records to the new Committee. The Committee also informed Bill Farrell that they no longer required the Common Room and the Office which were the original Settlement buildings and indeed where Bill and Betty Farrell still lived. In his diary Bill Farrell records, "This upset me very much for not only have I not been asked to remain (while I am still here) as the Honorary Warden, I have not even been co-opted on to nor asked to serve in any advisory way on their Committee and a plumber, with only two years user membership … is considered a fit and proper person to follow me and to take over 'the honour and office of the Warden' with all its responsibilities and duties. What have I been doing here for twenty three years? This is impossible."

Bill had received no salary since the end of March and was effectively bankrupt with an overdraft of £115 – ironically, the sum owed to him by the Trustees. The ultimate humiliation was to come on Tuesday 13th July. "…Today the wheel has come full circle and I have 'signed on the dole'. Twenty three years ago I came here to study the effects of unemployment and to do something to help unemployed people. I was young, healthy and fairly wealthy. Now I am only healthy but suppose must be very thankful for that. Time's whirligig is having a fine old spin round. …better men than I have drawn the dole and anyway it is my right and I have paid for it. Nevertheless there is a middle class horror of it in me somewhere. Its needs purgation."

This was the final insult. Bill needed to move on. Both he and Betty had been unsuccessfully applying for jobs for some while. Ironically Bill had been offered other posts prior to the closure of the Settlement, including Assistant Manager of the Garrison Theatre, Liverpool and resident warden for a new centre that the International Youth Centre in London proposed to set up - 'Eighteen

Bill & Betty Farrell with Michael the dog

Plus' - a series of cultural activities for the young servicemen and women as a 'pivot of international youth activities in Great Britain.' He had declined both opportunities, "my thoughts were for and of this Settlement, this child of ours and all the grand working class people who are now our friends and intimates and to whom, in all humbleness, I can say my wife and I mean so much. Can we desert them now? We are under no illusions and know that this place would just disappear now if we left. There then is our dilemma…"

Bill re-established contact with many of his acquaintances in the art and theatre worlds but his age appeared to be against him and, sadly, there is no record of him ever gaining further employment despite his huge breadth of knowledge and experience. After many disappointments, Betty was eventually appointed Headmistress of Abbotsley School in Huntingdonshire and the Farrells finally quit the Spennymoor Settlement on 30th December 1954. Bill Farrell left, an embittered man, with his long-planned novel, the story of the struggles of a young 1930s Spennymoor miner, forever unwritten. Some eight years later however, the Farrells were to return to their beloved North East. Betty Farrell, aged 62, retired from teaching in August 1962 as the Farrells had been offered the tenancy of a flat in Ormsby Hall, Middlesbrough. The owner Colonel James Pennyman, a close friend of theirs, had recently died and the Hall had been given to the National Trust. His widow Ruth Pennyman was to continue to live there and the Farrells became tenants of the Trust. Bill wrote with some delight to the Right Honourable Lord Kilmaine of the Pilgrim Trust "…we are to return to the North East where we left most of our friends in Spennymoor and all over the area." The Farrells had much in common with the Pennymans - they shared a love of the arts. Ruth herself was heavily involved in drama and mime and as early as the 1930s had set aside part of Ormsby Hall as an arts centre and headquarters for a theatre workshop. She went on to write, with Bill's encouragement, single-act plays which could be performed by small touring theatre companies. Hence it was apposite that Bill and Betty Farrell should end their days in these comfortable and stimulating surroundings.

The Farrells were to spend their final years together at Ormsby Hall, renewing acquaintances and enjoying the North Eastern culture until Bill's death in 1971. A moving and fitting tribute was paid to him by one of his successful Settlement members, the writer Sid Chaplin, in the obituary entitled 'A Man who cared'.

"Not only the old North-East of the depression and unemployment but the modern region with its new outlook and broader aspirations has lost a great mentor in Bill Farrell. He played a pivotal role in the development of a regional consciousness and the extraordinary thing is that this was done in the space of less than a quarter of a century and almost wholly by personal influence through classes and groups held in a couple of terrace houses which he and his helpers built themselves that constituted the Spennymoor Settlement. Virtually all which is now represented by Northern Arts [now Arts Council, North East] could be seen in embryo in the Settlement in those early days and successive generations of ordinary folk, like myself, found through Bill Farrell a highway to scholarship and the arts.

Bill Farrell was also a reader, a planter of trees, a geologist, an archaeologist and climber of mountains and a painter of considerable merit who had a compulsive urge to share his interests and enthusiasm with others. To be in his company was to be enlarged and to catch fire, to appreciate and to care – it was caring which brought him to Spennymoor in the first place.

50th Anniversary Celebration
L to R - Audrey Fisher, Daniel Storey, Ernst Brauer, Betty Farrell, Sid Chaplin, George Thompson

As one of the youngsters who came under his influence in the 30s I remember he and his settlement as representing manna in the wilderness. I know there are hundreds more, makers all, teachers, artists, actors and many others who owe their first start to him. They must feel as I do today a great gap in their lives and our hearts must go out to his active colleague and unfailing good companion in his work and achievements, his wife Betty."

chapter fifteen

The play must go on

'Granite' by Clemence Dane, 1954

" Man, in the beginning,
Look well, and take good heed of the ending."

Everyman, fifteenth century morality play

Undoubtedly the Settlement found itself in a parlous state from 1954 onwards. Although the books had been balanced at the end of the 1954 financial year, effectively with no income and a mounting overdraft, the institution was approaching bankruptcy. It is recorded that even the stalwarts of the Theatre Group were drifting away and at a typical meeting at the time only Muriel Lamb, Betty and Hazel Wendel, Bob Welch, Carrie Johnson, Cecily Milburn and Lily Banham attended. They were without direction and leadership and no play was being produced. Even the Sketching Club was in decline and many a Saturday passed without a single member turning up.

Set of 'The Mother' by Maxim Gorky, 1948

Betty Wendel was instrumental in ensuring the survival of the Theatre Group. She had been producing plays consistently at the Settlement since the 1950 production of Roy Russell's 'Return to Bedlam'. Betty went on to produce The Everyman Theatre Company's play 'Granite' by Clemence Dane. Performed in November 1954, this was the first production since the Settlement members had taken over total responsibility for both the building and its functions without paid help or grants from external funders as Betty Wendel explained in her programme notes. The Theatre Company members had realised, pragmatically, that if the group was to continue using the theatre they would have to support the new voluntary regime. Similarly, it is recorded that Bob Welch subsequently became Vice-Chairman and by 1956 he had taken on the role of Warden. Betty Wendel had called to see Bill Farrell, as he records in his diary on 13th August 1954, "...to discuss her own programme of possible plays for future production in my theatre. I am glad she does this for she is the only one now in the Company who has had any experience of production and as she has been my close collaborator, confidante, friend and fellow producer for some six or more years, she knows something of my ideas, philosophy and ideals as well as something of the real human history lying behind each brick and stick, each lamp and prop in my theatre. She will hold and I hope carry on something of the tradition."

In a similar way, determined Settlement member, teacher Muriel Lamb, went on to embrace all aspects of theatre craft. As well as being a keen artist in her own right. Muriel was known for her no nonsense approach to stage management and was a firm disciplinarian. Originally appearing as an actor she featured in the 1954 production of 'Granite' as Judith Morris. The Northern Echo of 12th November 1954 exclaimed "The play was a personal triumph for Miss Muriel Lamb who, for the whole play, was never off the stage, and gave a most dramatic presentation of a very difficult part. She received excellent support from Trevor Airey, Wilfred Jolly, John Bray and James Mason." By 1956 Muriel had moved on to be both set designer and producer of that year's performance of Gordon Glennon's 'Gathering Storm'.

In 1958, as well as staging four plays, the programme for the February production of 'Art and Mrs Bottle'- a play in three acts by Ben Levy and produced by Betty Airey - records that, in addition to the Sketching Group and the Theatre Company, the

Muriel Lamb

Settlement hosted both senior and junior Philatelic Groups under the guidance of Settlement President, Councillor Doctor Ernst Brauer, an Aero Modelling Group, a Chess Club, a Time and Motion Study Group, a Religion and Philosophy Class and a Musical Appreciation Society. The Musical Appreciation Society (the Music Group) was organised by Betty Wendel and met every Sunday evening in the theatre. Most of the great works of music were played on gramophone records, preceded by an appreciation of the work. Member Charles Bolton recalls, "The Group attempts to cover all important aspects of music, including in its compass opera, chamber, and ballet music drawn not only from the classical master but also from the more modern and unfamiliar composers – ranging from Bach and Beethoven to Arthur Bliss and Lennox Berkeley." The Settlement continued to foster musical ambition when, in 1963, four local lads, Kenny Potts, Donny Aston, Dave Roberts and Alan White – 'The Downbeats' - asked if they could use the Settlement to rehearse their pop music in return for free performances at the Settlement. 'The Downbeats' were to become known as 'The Blue Chips' under the same management as the Newcastle group 'The Animals' and experienced some chart success in 1966 with a number of releases. Drummer, Alan White, went on to play with John Lennon and eventually with the famous rock band 'Yes' – becoming, at one point, the highest paid drummer in the world.

Check Mate - Chess Club Members

The Spennymoor Choral Society was a popular and cohesive group in the Settlement. Audrey Fisher, music lover and choir member, later to become secretary of the group, recalls her first musical memories of the Spennymoor Settlement. "…I first came to the Settlement when a small child. Mrs Farrell used to have a music class on Saturday mornings. It was held in the building used by the St. John's Ambulance Service. She taught us to play musical instruments by following coloured notes on a blackboard." Of the Choir itself Audrey tells us, "…a lot of the men had been musicians with brass bands in the community and could therefore sing music as if their voices were instruments, as of course they were." She pays tribute to Dr. Brauer whom, she affirms, did so much for the Settlement and always managed to obtain assistance when it was needed. Over the years the Choir saw many changes, particularly in the dwindling numbers of male members, and to counter this it re-established itself and changed its name to the Settlement Choir. Members often gave concerts locally and went out into the community, entertaining at churches, hospitals and old people's homes etc. Audrey continues "…we had many happy times … We helped the Settlement in many ways - joining other classes, helping with jumble sales and even painting the Settlement walls and ceiling, selling tickets for the Drama Section and looking after the hall when on holiday."

These reminiscences are reinforced by fellow choir member Vera Williams who had joined the Settlement whilst still at school, initially as a member of the choir, but she tells us that she was encouraged to get involved in the life of the Settlement and went on to become Chairman. Vera is currently heavily committed to helping with funding for the regeneration project. A success story of the Settlement, the Choir went on to gain third prize in the BBC Radio Choir Northern Lights competition in 1980.

Originally a member of the Executive Committee, Settlement member Jim Storey was to emerge as a prominent figure in the organisation from the 1940s until his sudden death in 1999. He had no family tradition in the arts but was described by his widow, Pauline, as an extrovert by nature with an artistic flair. Jim was to become totally immersed in the whole ethos of the Settlement. From Business Manager to Honorary Secretary to Chairman and finally Warden, he made a significant contribution to the continued revival and long-term success of the organisation. Current Treasurer and Settlement stalwart, Malcolm Marsden, still refers to his former mentor as 'Mr Settlement'.

Ron & Audrey Fisher

"He was an actor, printer of posters, tickets and programmes, designed and painted sets, produced plays, provided properties etc. and spent hours doing unseen necessary manual tasks

Choir Members, L to R - Mrs. Wilkes, Mrs. Cummings, Mrs. Ball, Mrs. Scott, Mrs. Lowe, Mrs. Emmerson, Mrs. Cummings, Mrs. Fisher

to keep the building functional," Pauline Storey tells us, "whether it was sweeping floors, cleaning the toilet, putting out chairs, boarding up broken window panes or climbing a ladder with a substance to seal cracks on the outside of the flat roof in an attempt to prevent rain seeping into the building or opening and closing the premise for other groups … on call twenty four hours a day, seven days a week."

Like his mentor, Bill Farrell, Jim believed that the Settlement offered the man in the street a unique opportunity to access the arts through the experiences of acting, painting and singing. He was a consummate actor in his own right. Bill Farrell had recognised Jim's potential, inscribing on Jim's

programme for Gorky's 'The Mother' (in which Jim had played the part of Semyon)," Jimmy – you're a darling man and a potential artist – keep going." A review of Ibsen's 'Ghosts' in November 1966 stated, "The acting was really superb. I can recall no amateur acting that was performed so professionally as this, with each of the players giving realism to the character they portrayed. Edith Kirtley, as Mrs Alving and James B. Storey as Pastor Manders were outstanding in the way they brought their characters to life. … the whole production, designed and directed by Muriel Lamb, was impeccable and exceptionally well performed."

Such was his passion for the Settlement that after Jim's death, his wife Pauline and close family members and friends joined as Settlement members to follow on from Jim's lifelong commitment and love for the institution. They continue to fundraise on the Settlement's behalf and have even become members of the Executive Committee, Pauline currently being Vice Chairman and daughter, Louise Edgar, carries on the family tradition too in her role as Vice President. Following Jim's death, the next production by the Everyman Theatre Company in March 2000 was dedicated to his memory.

Jim Storey, 1950s (Photo courtesy of Pauline Storey)

chapter sixteen

The curtain rises

Cast of "Murder Deferred' by Stuart Ready 2003

"… this theatre is our own roof-tree, here is no exclusion, no high art or low but only the best in which we all can share."

Sid Chaplin

By the late 1950s the Theatre Group had re-established itself and was regularly producing several plays a year. Paradoxically whilst there had been a shortage of male actors, there were many men involved in stage management and on the technical side of theatre productions, several of whom were persuaded to tread the boards! One such was current Treasurer Malcolm Marsden. He originally joined the Philatelic Society in the late 1950s and later helped technicians Ian Wilson and George Bushell as third electrician operating the fire effects in the 'Piper of Orde'. In 1962 he was asked by the then producer Muriel Lamb to play the part of

Horace Bunce in the comedy 'One of those Days' by Kent Richards and so began to appear both on and off stage. Encouraged by Jim Storey, Malcolm began to build and later design sets and arrange the lighting plot. He also took on the role of stage manager for many of the productions. Malcolm was to become the first ever Settlement actor to cause a production to be delayed because "he was flying in from the West End." The West End in question was his company's West End London offices where Malcolm had been conducting urgent business. Jim Storey deliberately gave no inkling of this when he jokingly informed the waiting audience of the reason for the late start of the play.

'Put that light out' June 2005. Cast list:- Malcolm Marsden, Audrey Hartnell, Barry Barker, Marion Jackson, Malcolm Stamp, Sylvia Dobson, Dave Acock and Melenie Welsh.

In the early 1970s, with Malcolm as Secretary and Jim Storey as Chairman, Settlement funds were low and the fabric of the building was in desperate need of repair. The members decided to cut their losses, dispose of Pilgrim House, the original Settlement building, in exchange for Freehold Revisionary of the Scout Hut, now known as the Annexe – making all Settlement property freehold.

Fortunately, the Settlement was able to draw on the expertise of member Terry Robson, a qualified solicitor, to advise on this complex negotiation. Terry had joined the theatre group in the 1960s and was widely respected as a talented actor. He was ultimately to become President, a post which he held for a number of years until his retirement due to ill health.

The cast of 'Black Chiffon' by Lesley Storm, 1987

The Settlement membership was in decline at this period and the number of groups had been reduced. The Scout Hut housed the Weightlifting and later the Table Tennis Clubs but was under-utilised. A member of St. John's Ambulance, Malcolm Marsden, had seen with some despair, their headquarters compulsorily purchased to make way for a new doctors' surgery. This left the Brigade homeless with nowhere to store its equipment. Despite having received £2,000 in compensation, they found themselves with insufficient funds to secure another home. It was Malcolm's suggestion that all St. John's members become Settlement members to enable them to secure a permanent meeting place in the Settlement Annexe. This pragmatic solution was of mutual benefit. Spennymoor Town Council agreed to fund the upgrading of the Annexe and hence a new Settlement activity, the St. John's Ambulance Brigade, was born.

During the 1980s the Settlement continued to struggle financially but the Theatre Group remained viable despite the shortage of male members. Current Secretary, Marion Jackson, joined around this time and, apart from two shows, has appeared in every production since 1978. She made her first appearance playing the role of Nanny in the psychological drama 'Black Chiffon' by Lesley Storm.

Tribute must be paid to Marion who has dedicated her free time and effort to ensure that 'the play must go on'. Not only has she appeared on stage, she has worked as front-of-house, fund-raised tirelessly, addressed thousands of envelopes and penned hundreds of letters, all in a bid to make sure that the people of Spennymoor would not forget the legacy and importance of the Settlement and its building to the cultural, educational and economic past of the town. Together with others of the Executive Committee, including current Chairman Dave Acock, Marion has been at the vanguard of the initiative to secure the funding to ensure that the Settlement has a future especially the refurbishment of the mainstay of the Settlement – Bill Farrell's theatre.

Their love for the theatre over the years is admirably demonstrated by the loyalty of its members, many of whom recall Bill Farrell with affection and respect. Membership of the Theatre Group meant such a lot to Lillian Whitehead who was to remain a member for thirty seven years, playing many varied roles, as did the quiet-natured Betty Chisholm. Current President, Sylvia Dobson, first appeared on stage in the 1950s and has continued her successful acting career for over half a century! Her first review appeared on 4th February 1954 when the Auckland Chronicle reported, " Sylvia Dobson's portrayal of the quick-witted social-climbing daughter, Florrie, was played with vivacity and the right amount of petulant, spurious religiosity." Elsie Hands, later to become Elsie McCann, both acted and helped backstage,

'Gaslight' by Patrick Hamilton 1960 performance

keen to undertake any task required of her. In 1977 whilst helping with the lighting during a production of 'Gaslight' Elsie is especially remembered for an amusing incident. The play called for the leading actress to light a series of four 'gaslights' to heighten the drama at a pivotal point in the play. Elsie's job was to ensure synchronicity. This she achieved but unfortunately, confusing stage left with stage right, lit the lights in exactly the reverse sequence to the actress, bringing an unusual element of comedy to Patrick Hamilton's high drama. Despite this gaffe, Elsie assumed the 'mantle' of Treasurer for a number of years.

In the tradition of Bill Farrell, Settlement member Malcolm Stamp penned his own play, 'Put That Light Out', in June 2005 in commemoration of the sixtieth anniversary of the ending of The Second World War. This was something of a departure from the 'Everyman Theatre' trademark of drama, comedy and tragedy and introduced audience participation with the singing of war-time songs. The play took the form of a spoof radio show based on 'ITMAR' and the programme notes announced that "due to war restrictions there would only be one seat between five adults." In the

Set of 'Murder Deferred' 2003

spirit of the send-up, author Malcolm Stamp dedicated the production to his father "who has managed to miss it!" The script was still being refined during the actual run! A display of wartime memorabilia enhanced the production.

Bill Farrell's legacy was to inspire yet another generation. Theatre member Melenie Welsh's son, Adam, on a visit to the Settlement, was inveigled to join the youth theatre and went on to perform in the lottery funded production 'The Tree That Held Up the Sky'. This experience was instrumental in persuading him that his future lay in an acting career and he went on to graduate, with honours, from the Royal Academy of Dramatic Arts (RADA).

At a more prosaic level, it is testimony to the affection with which the members held the theatre that, in 2003, members of the group personally made a contribution to ensure the restoration of the scenery which had been in use for over sixty years and which was in a deplorable state. Malcolm Marsden, Barry Barker, John Robinson and Ryan Lamb set about stripping and repairing all the theatre flats and replacing the canvases. These refurbished flats were first used for the play 'Murder Deferred' in 2003 to great acclaim as the audience applauded the set instantly the curtain opened. Barry Barker has also been instrumental in updating the stage management methods to incorporate new computer technology, particularly with regard to special sound effects. He went on to play leading roles including in 'Ladies in Retirement' in 2006 before moving on to join the St. David's group of players.

Malcolm Stamp & Sylvia Dobson in 'Put that light out' by Malcolm Stamp, June 2005

In recent years innovative methods have been used to increase funds and maximise profits. During the scene changes a buffet for the audience was introduced, allowing a premium to be added to the price of admission tickets. Not only has this proved popular with the audience, it has almost doubled each show's profits. In addition the introduction of a Gift Aid scheme to members has capitalised on some of the donated income since 2002.

chapter seventeen

Encore

Dave Acock & Marion Jackson discuss the plans (Photo courtesy of The Northern Echo)

"Houses built with hands may come and go, but theatre – that living, growing yet timeless structure – we have always with us."

Sid Chaplin

The Spennymoor Settlement

For too many years the voluntary organisation behind the Settlement had manfully struggled to maintain the fabric and the buildings on a shoe-string budget. Most of the repairs, out of necessity, had been on a make–do and mend basis often using materials discarded from the members' own homes. This self sufficiency of course had been part of the ethos behind the Settlement since its inception in 1931. Amongst those who appreciated the significance of a visionary social experiment that had its beginnings in the desperate days of the depression of the 1930s there undoubtedly had been a determination for the institution to survive. The original experiment had encapsulated all the basic requirements of subsistence existence within the microcosm of life that is theatre craft.

Cast of 'The Caretaker' by George Shiels, 1949

Ironically this was the era of all-encompassing art movements based on the original Arts and Crafts Movement of the turn of the previous century - the Art Deco Movement with its exponents in the Bauhaus in Berlin, the Wiener Werkstatte in Vienna and the Rennie Mackintosh School of Art in Glasgow - where literature, architecture, furniture, textiles, sculpture and imagery were all brought together under the umbrella of the central philosophy of 'design'. Perhaps this is from where Bill Farrell drew his inspiration and from where he modelled Spennymoor Settlement, basing it around 'the arts'.

Stylistically, Art Deco was bright and geometrical and used modern materials with a hard-edged, shiny simplicity giving a spacious sense of opulence and hence only lay in the domain of the upper classes. This was in stark contrast to the reality of the grime and desperation of the working class. Were the fundamental principles transferable? Could the unemployed miner in County Durham be taught to survive through the medium of the arts? Was this the ideology behind Bill Farrell's original thoughts on Spennymoor rather than simple pragmatism? A legacy, the Spennymoor Settlement, has been left to us that many feel passionately should not just be preserved by fossilising it in time but should be allowed to flourish and continue its pioneering pathway in the field of 'arts for the working man'.

The importance of the Settlement's legacy can be appreciated at a personal level from an interview with Mrs Jean Alker who now lives in Redditch to where she and her husband Chris moved in 1957. Both were Settlement members and both appeared in plays in the late 1940s and early 1950s – Jean in just one or two but Chris was a regular performer appearing many times with Edith Kirtley and Iris Bray, both of whom Jean remembers as being excellent actresses. Jean also recalls the W.E.A. archaeology classes run by a tutor from Bishop

Jim Storey with Ron and Jean Akers and Bill and James Mason at a weekend theatre school (Photo courtesy of Pauline Storey)

Auckland who would take them to visit sites in his car and who encouraged all the group to write dissertations which went on exhibition in Durham. But what was the lasting Settlement legacy for the Alkers who attended the Settlement because they were interested in education and were in search of cultural activities? The answer was easy - good and stimulating conversation and lasting friendships. After over half a century of midland life Spennymoor is still home – a home where there are friends to be visited as often as possible. It wasn't until the Alkers arrived in a bereft Redditch that they fully appreciated the rich vein of culture that the Settlement had provided.

Perhaps it was thoughts of this nature that persuaded the Settlement Committee to once again try for resources to allow the institution to continue. The practical reality was, however, that the buildings were becoming unsafe. This led to the idea of applying for funding. It was first discussed in 2003. Emergency repairs had had to be undertaken when it was discovered that the corners of the theatre roof were literally falling off. A feasibility study was commissioned from Messrs Kataky and Kelly from Sedgefield Borough Council and thus the full extent of the dilapidation was finally appreciated. Without this study, the building would have had to close for health and safety reasons. This decision would have been the responsibility of the borough council, so the choice of two of their officers as agents was, in retrospect, a shrewd move.

The process of bidding for funding was not straightforward. Much of the planning and design had to be reconsidered on several occasions to comply with the changing regulations, necessitating the repeated redrawing and resubmission of plans. The definitive project to refurbish the theatre was eventually costed at £168,000. The bulk of this money, £118,000, was to come from the Local Improvement Programme (LIPS). This figure was revised upwards to £141,000 in the light of the Disability and Discrimination Act, Health and Safety considerations and unforeseen structural difficulties.

This grant still meant that the Settlement members had to find £50,000 to reach the funding target for the building itself. Katy Banner, Sedgefield Borough's Arts Officer, submitted a successful bid to the Lottery Heritage Fund for £50,000 towards building renovation and the production of this book on the history and significance of the Spennymoor Settlement, together with an educational programme. The original funders, The Pilgrim Trust, allocated £25,000 payable on receipt of the Architect's Certificate. Other funders included The Sir James Knott's Trust, Sherburn Hospital Trust, Durham Masonic Lodges, Spennymoor Rotary Club and

Cast of 'Ladies in Retirement' 2006

Barclays Bank. The members themselves raised £10,000. Significant funds for site clearance and garden refurbishment, including reinstating Dr Brauer's rose garden, based on an original design by Bill Farrell, came from County Durham Environmental Trust and specific funding was obtained for stage lighting from the Arts Council.

The theatre from its inception in 1939 was always proud of its facilities, particularly its stage lighting, which was state of the art when the building was new. Bill Farrell would boast that there was no better theatre lighting between Middlesbrough and Newcastle. In replacing the original lighting to return it to 'state of the art', a legacy from the original installation is to be kept - the switch panel from 1939 with its row upon row of elegant brass switches will still adorn the theatre wall stage left.

It was decided that tiered seating would provide the best viewing for the theatre audience, but this came at a price. To accommodate this plan the walls

Peter Bell with the original lighting board

supporting the wooden floor needed bolstering bringing with it a significant additional cost for the whole seating project. Much of this was met by the foresighted action of three local councillors - Andy Gray, John Kahn and Andrew Smith - who collectively donated their council 'Private Initiative Fund' to specifically fund this aspect of the project. This combined donation was gratefully received by the committee.

The £10,000 funding from the Settlement's own members almost harked back to the original Settlement days when bags of toffee were sold to raise capital for the theatre. Members staged coffee mornings each Saturday. Various other methods of fundraising were as diverse as car boot sales, beetle drives, table top sales, raffles, the Spennyknit Knitting and Crochet Group, charity quiz nights and the 'buy a brick scheme', promising those who bought a brick for £5 the receipt of a commemorative certificate and the inclusion of their name on the list of donors which is to be displayed in the Settlement building. All this was done under the aegis of the Spennymoor Settlement Regeneration Fund. The sum achieved bears testimony to the determination and inventiveness of the membership and gives the same sense of striving towards self-sufficiency that underpinned the original Settlement ethos.

After several false dawns the work on the theatre refurbishment commenced on 7th July 2008 with a twelve week time-frame and an expected completion date of mid-September 2008. After the tendering process, Manners Builders, an old established company from Bishop Auckland

Robert Heslop - Still Life, Oil, n.d.

with over one hundred years of experience in building renovation, were appointed as the main contractors. This seems to have been an inspired choice as the committee are fulsome in their praise for the contractors and Chairman Dave Acock tells us, "From management down, through design they are all a pleasure to work with and whilst the men themselves are grafters they will stop to explain to the inquisitive public what they are doing." The quality and detail of the renovation of the Grade 2 listed building delights Dave Acock who is keen to point out the care with which the brickwork and the decoration around the windows have been matched and how the facsimile of Tisa Hess's original sculpture above the entrance boldly announces a fresh welcome to all.

Members had already begun to recognise the necessity to collect and collate historical records and memorabilia pertaining to the Settlement's past. Local historian and author, Bob Abley had been approached and appointed as official archivist to the Settlement. With his knowledge and experience of new technology and electronic data storage, Bob has done sterling work to date in organising, preserving and documenting photographs and ephemera in an electronically-retrievable form for future generations and students of social history to access and to consult.

The committee feels sufficiently confident of the contractor's ability to meet the deadline that already activities within the Settlement building are planned for October 2008. It seems the inaugural event may well be a Quiz Night in mid-October together with an exhibition of Settlement photographs, curated by Bob Abley. True to the traditions of the Settlement, The Everyman Players are in rehearsal with the play 'Poor Geoffrey' which is due for production in November.

Chairman Dave Acock can foresee many other potential activities for the Settlement to host, including the Tudhoe and Spennymoor History Society, a fortnightly family history course with internet access to ancestry websites, St John's Ambulance and the Art Group who both already use the annexe on Mondays, young pop groups, brass bands, variety nights and, of course, continuing drama in the form of The Everyman Players and the Bishop Auckland Theatre Hooligans youth theatre group. Echoing the days of the Pitman's Academy will be a rolling programme of art and photographic exhibitions in the theatre auditorium.

Whilst it is planned to use the buildings as soon as they are re-commissioned, no date has been set for the official opening. This will take place before 31st March 2009, however, as this is the date when responsibilty is transferred from Sedgefield Borough Council to the new unitary authority of Durham County Council. David Acock feels it would be appropriate for the opening ceremony to be performed by a member of royalty and that this person be the present Prince of Wales, His Royal Highness Prince Charles. This, Dave Acock suggests, would complete a cycle of royal interest given the concern shown to the Settlement by the then Prince of Wales, Prince Edward, in 1934. The opening ceremony will represent the third incarnation of the Spennymoor Settlement.

But what of its future? Is there a new 'clientele' who will want to assume the mantle of education through the arts for the working man and to pass it on to yet another generation? Time has moved on and although the mass unemployment which inflicted Spennymoor in the 1930s has gone, there are clouds on the economic horizon and recently-announced job losses will undoubtedly impact on the town's prosperity. The educational needs and provisions have changed as have leisure activities, but where else can the inquisitive individual sample as diverse a range of practical and creative skills locally within one organisation? Whilst nostalgia and a sense of history, even heroic survival, play important roles in this theatre of life the final act of the drama is far from being written. There is a vision to extend the Settlement further with perhaps rebuilding a two-storey block with a dedicated art studio on the site of the annexe and

70th Anniversary Exhibition, Bishop Auckland Town Hall, 2001
L to R - Bill Mason, Edith Kirtley, Arnold Hadwin, Rene Chaplin, Ruby Murray, Tom McGuinness and Norman and Sarah Cornish

Bill Farrell at his easel 1930s (Photo courtesy of Rene Chaplin)

even to re-acquire the original shops in King Street to form a quadrangle for an all-encompassing arts and educational centre. Whilst these determinations are at present visions, almost dreams, it was a man armed with little more than determination, dreams and a vision that brought hope to a town where there was only despair and showed Spennymoor 'A Way to the Better'.

postscript

Ironically, although the Settlement Movement would appear to be in decline because the social conditions which led to the foundation of the movement apparently no longer exist, there has been a recent upsurge in interest and a revival of "the oldest, most radical and most neglected model for helping the poor in the cities – the Victorian settlement - which is proving an ideal partner in community renewal schemes," states John Cunningham in his Guardian article of 11th April 2001. He goes on, "Settlements had a mission to bring about social improvement through interaction between their young educated helpers – the future elite, who often became passionate reformers – and those in need. Over time, the approach fell from fashion, but the social ills they set out to tackle over a century ago are still around, although in contemporary guises. Now, for the first time since the 1960s and 1970s, when settlements lost direction, saw incomes shrink and were eclipsed by the trend for vociferous community action, there are plans for expansion."

The University of Surrey and The London School of Economics are both planning a new graduate community-work course based on the settlement model. It is not only universities that are reinvestigating this model, local councils too are taking a fresh look at partnership possibilities. Its attraction to local authorities is that settlements provide direct services, but can cross the divide and provide support for small emerging community and ethnic groups. There is a scheme to deliver neighbourhood renewal plans through this model in Newcastle upon Tyne and Tower Hamlets in East London. This resurgence of interest in the settlement model is not confined to new schemes but also impacts on long-established settlement institutions including a huge scheme involving the Birmingham Settlement which has twenty three separate projects covering the full range of community services and working in partnership with over two hundred local organisations.

Perhaps historically of most significance, however, is a project proposed for Toynbee Hall itself. Reverend Professor Luke Geoghegan, Warden of Toynbee Hall, states, "We are going to recreate our original roots and start a residential community for bright, young, talented people who want to go on and change the world" – direct heirs of Bill Farrell's original 'shock brigade'! The idea is that the students will continue with their careers but will live in Toynbee Hall, working as volunteers in the evenings and at weekends with the less-fortunate members of the local community. Rather than see this as a 'think tank', Professor Geoghegan prefers to call it a 'do tank', with a direct hands-on approach. The first fifteen residents were appointed in September 2001 and now there are over seventy residents extending help to groups as diverse as local elderly Bengalis or persistent young offenders. Whilst the clientele may have changed from Bill Farrell's time the principle, that of giving the 'educated' the opportunity to help the less fortunate in society, remains the same.

Robert McManners and Gillian Wales

Appendix 1: Productions by Settlement Players

The Cradle Song	G. Martinez Sierra		1934
The Playboy of the Western World	J.M. Synge	Nov	1935
Everyman	Anon	Mar	1939
The Lover	G. Martinez Sierra in rehearsal	Mar	1940
The Stronger	A. Strindberg		1940
The Coventry Nativity Play	Anon	Dec	1940
The Three Stooges	Scouts for Scouts	Apr	1940
Putting a Reef in Granny	Scouts	Apr	1940
*Ladies in Waiting	C. Campion	May	1940
Rosmersholm	H. Ibsen	May/June	1940
Hedda Gabler	H. Ibsen	Sept	1940
Distant Point	A. Afinogenev	June	1942
Gabriel	Ruth Pennyman and W.G. Farrrell	June	1944
Pound on Demand	Sean O'Casey	June	1944
The Sword of the Spirit	R. Swingler	June	1944
The Siren	S. Purnell and W.G. Farrell		1944
First Class Journey, Single	Scouts for Scouts		1944
Moonlight Rhapsody	J. Maddison		1944
Closing Time	S. Purnell		1944
Inga	A. Glebov		1944
They Came to a City	J.B. Priestley	Mar	1945
They Came to a City	J.B. Priestley	June	1945
The New Gossoon	George Shiels	Nov	1946
Mother	Maxim Gorky	Nov	1948
The Sacred Flame	W. Somerset Maugham	Dec	1948

*this was the first production of a full-length play in the Everyman Theatre

Unto the End	James Graham	Apr/May	1949
The Caretakers	George Shiels	Nov	1949
The Golden Fleece	J.B. Priestley	Dec	1949
Return to Bedlam	Roy Russell	Mar	1950
The Devil	Ben Levy	May	1950
The Linden Tree	J.B Priestley	Nov	1950
The Three-cornered Moon	Gertrude Tonkonogy	Dec	1950
Easter	A. Strindberg	Mar	1951
The Long Mirror	J.B. Priestley	Apr	1951
Quinn's Secret	George Shiels	June	1951
Return to Tyassi	Ben Levy	Nov	1951
Juno and the Paycock	Sean O'Casey	Mar	1952
The Seven Sleepers	Robert Gittings	June	1952
The Corn is Green	Emlyn Williams	Dec	1952
The Holly and the Ivy	Wynyard Browne	Mar	1953
Message for Margaret	James Parish	July	1953
Sheppey	W. Somerset Maugham	Jan	1954
Granite	Clemence Dane	Nov	1954
The Late Christopher Bean	Emlyn Williams	Feb	1955
Blithe Spirit	Noel Coward	May	1955
Robert's Wife	St John Ervine	Oct	1955
Mungo's Mansion	Walter Macken	Feb	1956
Gathering Storm	Gordon Glennon	May	1956
Captain Carvallo	Denis Cannan	Nov	1956
Someone Waiting	Emlyn Williams	April	1957
Fools Rush In	Kenneth Horne	June	1957
Art and Mrs Bottle	Ben Levy	Feb	1958
Duet for Two Hands	Mary Haley Bell	May	1958
The Same Sky	Yvonne Mitchell	Oct	1958
But Once a Year	Falkland L. Carey	Dec	1958
Dangerous Corner	J.B. Priestley	May	1959

All for Mary	H. Brooke & K. Bannerman	Oct	1959
Bell, Book and Candle	John Van Druten	Dec	1959
Gaslight	Patrick Hamilton	Feb	1960
No Escape	Rhys Davies	July	1960
Hippo Dancing	Robert Morley	Nov	1960
Mungo's Mansion	Walter Macken		1961
Corinth House	Pamela Hansford- Johnson	Dec	1961
One of Those Days	Kent Richards	June	1962
We Must Kill Toni	Ian Stuart Black	Oct	1962
The Piper of Orde	Rosamunde Pilcher and Charles C. Gardiner	Apr	1963
Your Obedient Servant	Diana Morgan	June	1963
Serious Charge	Philip King	Nov	1963
Billy Liar	Keith Waterhouse and Willis Hall	June	1964
Crime on Goat Island	Ugo Betti	Dec	1964
Pound on Demand	Sean O'Casey	May	1965
Margaret	Eve Bannister	May	1965
Sganarelle	Moliere	May	1965
Breath of Spring	Peter Coke	June	1965
We must kill Toni	Ian Stuart Black	Oct	1965
Ghosts	H. Ibsen	Nov	1966
Celebration	Keith Waterhouse and Willis Hall	Apr	1967
The Country Boy	John Murphy	July	1967
Sit Down a Minute Adrian	Jevan Brandon-Thomas	Dec	1967
Christ's Resurrection (cycle of mystery plays)		May	1968
Doctor in the House	Ted Willis	Oct	1968
Satellite Story	Anthony Booth	June	1969
The Happiest Days of Your Life	John Dighton	Nov	1969
The Late Edwina Black	William Dinner and William Morum	June	1970
Lucky Strike		Dec	1970

Ring for Catty	Patrick Cargill and Jack Beale	Sept	1971
Strike Happy	Duncan Greenwood	May	1972
All things Bright and Beautiful	Keith Waterhouse and Willis Hall	Aug	1972
The House on the Cliff	George Batson	Dec	1972
Corinth House	Pamela Hansford-Johnson	Sept	1974
Lucky for Some	John Dole	Feb	1975
Thriller of the Year	Glyn Jones	Nov	1975
Breath of Spring	Peter Coke	Jan	1976
Tangled web	Patricia Gordon	July	1976
Gaslight	Patrick Hamilton	Oct	1977
Murder Deferred	Stuart Ready	Nov	1978
Beside the Seaside	Leslie Sands	June	1980
Basin Full of the Briny	Leslie Sands	Nov	1980
Black Chiffon	Lesley Storm	June	1981
Blithe Spirit	Noel Coward	June	1982
And This Was Odd	Kenneth Horne	May	1983
Ladies in Retirement	Edward Percy and Reginald Denham	Dec	1983
Thriller of the Year	Glyn Jones	May	1984
Breath of Spring	Peter Coke	Dec	1984
Corinth House	Pamela Hansford -Johnson	July	1985
The Paying Guest	Peter Assinder	April	1989
The Little Evenings	Diana Morgan	April	1989
The Last Act	Myra Williams	Dec	1989
Tangled Web	Patricia Gordon	June	1990
Thriller of the year	Glyn Jones		1991
Beautiful for Ever	Glyn Jones	May	1993
A Funeral Tea Trilogy	Pat Wilson et al	July	1994
Blithe Spirit	Noel Coward	May	1995
Murder Mistaken	Janet Green	Nov	1995

The Man Born to be King: Part 3:

A Certain Nobleman	Dorothy L. Sayers	May	1996
The Late Edwina Black	William Dinner and William Morum	June	1996
How Now Hecate?	Martyn Coleman	Oct	1996
Radio Days	Michael Hampel	July	1997
Breath of Spring			1998
Farndale Avenue Housing Estate Townswomen Guild in a Murder Mystery Play		Mar	2000
Our Husband	Brandon Fleming	Oct/Nov	2002
The Plot Thickens	Mark Langham	Oct/Nov	2002
Housekeeper Wanted	Philip King and Falkland L. Cary	Oct/Nov	2002
Murder Deferred	Stuart Ready	July	2003
Farndale Avenue Townswomen's Guild's Haunted Through Lounge	David McGillivary and Walter Zerlin Jnr	June	2004
Thespians in Trouble	David Tristran	Mar	2005
Put That Light Out	Malcolm Stamp	June	2005
The Legend	Philip Johnson	Nov	2005
A Respectable Funeral	Jimmie Chin	Nov	2005
The Clouded Star – Nativity Play at St Paul's Church		Dec	2005
The Murder of P C Rook	David Acock	Mar	2006
Ladies in Retirement	Edward Percy and Reginald Denham	Aug/Sept	2006
The Murder of P C Rook (at Bishop Auckland Town Hall)	David Acock	Oct	2006
Murder Mystery Eveneing: Funeral Tea (at St. David's Church, Tudhoe)			2007
Murder Mystery Evening		Oct	2007

Appendix 2: "… way to the better…" being some account of the Founding, Achievements and Aims of the Spennymoor Settlement

by W.G. Farrell

Founded by the Pilgrim Trust in 1931 and controlled, in those early days, by the British Association of Residential Settlements, the Settlement at Spennymoor has worked towards its own "liquidation" as a Settlement. That may be overstatement, but it is true, essentially, and, in either case, it commended itself to this writer for its dramatic effectiveness.

Those were the bad days of long continued unemployment, and the Settlement was founded in the hope that it might do something, however small, to study, make known, and if possible to alleviate some of the social evils arising from the economic disaster which hit Durham County as badly, if not worse, than any other of the industrial areas.

"If way to the better there be, it exacts a full look at the Worst." Thomas Hardy's dictum was the basis of the early investigations and it led the Settlement into some queer places and, as experience followed experience, into a more and more shocked awareness of the problem. Enough time, paper and ink has been used in the painting of that picture and I do not propose to try to do it again.

It must suffer here to say that in the early days of its life the Settlement was forced to realise that it must begin, not as a Red Cross unit, with an ambulance for the fallen, but as a belligerent, to take part in a War that might never end, a War that killed children slowly, that drove men and women to dullness, despair, degradation, in some cases, death by their own hands, a War waged by those who would preserve a social and economic system, which, the longer it lived, could by the very nature of its structure, only perpetuate that War, and in the end the cataclysm which has now, for a time, most surely ended mass unemployment, but which has not ended the spiritual and economic poverty of mankind.

The new Settlement entered that conflict carrying little or no armaments other than the flame of a belief in the sanctity and needs of the individual. But it had to begin by trying to convince the army in which it had enlisted that it was a good and worthwhile comrade.

The Settlement then was founded and maintained by money from a private trust. It could, and would not have been founded otherwise. It was meant to serve and, because of its financial security, was enabled to serve the people, but many other people themselves suspected it for they believed that nobody from "the outside" could be actuated by purely altruistic motives towards them. In view of all that had gone before who now dares says that their suspicions were unjustified? The '26' is still remembered in Durham. That then was the first thing which had to be faced, and, in those days, it was sufficient to deter many responsible public men from assisting the work, and indeed a number of them actively opposed it. Ignorance of the kind of work done by the so-called Voluntary Social Services was at the root of all. An isolated few understood what was contemplated but not enough to justify the handing over of its control to a purely local council or committee, and the Settlement remained controlled from 'the outside'. Questions of policy and direction were left to the Warden who formed a small local committee for advisory purposes only. Today, however, some local working class people are members of the Council and Committee which holds some power, but even those bodies are controlled by the fact that the main source of income is still outside the area. And for so long as the money has to come from 'the outside' just for so long will the people themselves be unable to exercise real power and control, and just for so long will the Settlement remain a place where people from 'the outside' settled, and its democratic basis will be open to question. And that is the situation which the Settlement itself dislikes, and which it must earnestly desire to see 'liquidated' so long as it is done and taken over, by people who really understand its philosophy, and its purpose.

Only peak moments in its history can be indicated here. In the beginning no adequate premises were available so the Warden and his wife settled in and over an empty shop, opened their doors wide and invited a suspicious leisurefull populace to come in. Far too many did. There was not room for them all and so came the decision which coloured the whole of the settlement's subsequent history. Inadequate accommodation made it impossible to *do things for many hundreds of people so it was decided to do those things the settlers themselves liked, and could do best, with those others of their neighbours who liked and wished to do the same things.* In passing it seems well to note that there is a world of difference between those two small italicised prepositions.

Lack of accommodation then, and, be it said, preference also, dictated a qualitative rather than a quantitative method. This palliative, the "club to keep the people quiet" method was just not possible, even if it had been wanted. The Warden, who, amongst other things, was a painter and theatre artist with very definitive views, and whose wife was similarly gifted, then decided to begin by organising groups of people to engage in such and similar creative activities. A Play-Reading Group and a Sketching Club were formed, and a Carpenter's and Cobbler's Shop was stocked and opened. Political and Social Science Classes, a Folk Dancing Class, and a Scout Troop and Children's Play Centre (for lack of a Real Nursery School) were also begun. Only those who were anxious to do one or more of those things were admitted into membership and, most important of those early decisions was that employed persons, as well as unemployed, were welcomed for it was obvious that segregation would only lead to further and more disastrous differences.

And so the Settlement came to life with a body of some three hundred men, women, and children members from whom it was hoped to form, at some future date, a shock brigade of trained and socially conscious people to join in the fight against the real enemies of society elsewhere. That did, and still does happen. Men and women students learned something of the parts they ought to play in society in the Settlement classes, and in the discussions in the Common Room, and go out to play those parts, as responsible citizens, in local government, and in social and political affairs. But how much easier all this would have been if Durham, like some other Universities, had had its School of Social Science, and how much quicker and easier it will be when such a School is established can only be known to those who do take an active part in affairs now, and who know how very few trained people there are here in County Durham, The foundation of such a school is one of the major aims of the Spennymoor Settlement. It will have to come and its students must be drawn from, young men and women of the pit villages who intend to remain, work and use their knowledge and training in the parent coalfield. Incentive to remain? Yes, but that this is another story, and one which I cannot tell here. Something of it may perhaps be dimly seen through the other ideas detailed here. The need is great. How and from whence it will be met? Again more of that later, if only indirectly and by implication.

It has been stated above that the Settlement attracted to itself those who wished to take part in some kind of creative activity, and it would seem it had forgotten those all too many others who did not wish, or could not join in such things. It never did, and has not now forgotten them, but it has always realised that first things must come first. Shock troops were and are those first things, and as yet the call up of that class is by no means complete. It would also appear that the Settlement forgot about all those other people living in different parts of the coalfield. But this was not so, for the Warden toured the county and helped to organise some thirty or more of what in 1938 came to be known as Social Service Centres and which he imbued with some of the Settlement's ideas.

The triumphs and failures of those first ten years were many. Following on the lines of 'Toynbee Hall' the Pioneer Settlement, Spennymoor entered into every aspect of the life about it. It could not ally itself to any particular creed or party but it worked with all progressive movements, and sent its members to work in their fields. Young men and women were sent on their way to greater things, to Ruskin, and other 'Workers' Colleges', while other groups conducted social researches, the results of one of which were later quoted in the House of Commons. It has spoken for, and advocated by its own practical work, the establishment of Nursery Schools, unhappily, so far, without much success. It has also formulated its own theories of Educational practices.

In 1938/9, substantially helped by grants from the Commissioner for the Special Areas, and gifts from old professional theatre friends of the Warden, and by the members' own efforts, it built its own 'Everyman Theatre'. Today this still carries on. Little has stopped as a direct result of the War, but much has been taken on, or extended to meet the special conditions now prevailing. It argues that this War is being waged for just those very things for which it stands, and does not intend to let those things die because at the moment they have no glamour for the multitude. One important addition to its activities is the formation of an '18 Plus' Club, a club of young, thinking people, which promises well for the future. Many members are in the forces, gathering and giving new impressions, and collecting and sharing new experiences. They will come back to us at Spennymoor, and they will not be the same young people who went away!

Volumes of the first hand experience are in the possession of the Settlement and are all of real value. Little of it can be mentioned now but perhaps something of the most important and most interesting item should be indicated. The Settlement rediscovered and later proved to many men and women of Durham County that they themselves are not only the 'tough guys' the outside world thinks them to be, but that they are also endowed with talents for painting, sculpture, verse and song making and for the theatre crafts in particular. Those gifts, if wrongly developed, and badly focused, can be and indeed all too often have become drugs to the owners, poison to the spectators, and serious drags on the wheels of social progress. Rightly focused, trained in a school with a social purpose behind it, and exercised in the sure and certain knowledge that such gifts are sacred and only held in trust for the service of the people, they can be of incalculable value in the stormy days of social change that are before us. The Settlement knows this well, and while it is colloquially known as the 'Pitmen's Academy' exhibits and sells its pictures and work everywhere the members know that their primary job is to portray the grandeurs, and the littlenesses of Durham folk so that all, and particularly Durham folk themselves, may come to know that even though they may be of the earth earthy, they are the very salt of the earth, and are proud of it. The Theatre too is used to the end that revitalising entertainment may be given by Durham folk. It is not, and never has been, thought of as a place where 'Amateurs' play, but as a place where a really serious job has to be done, where native Dramatists, Actors, Poets, Painters, Singers, Dancers, Carpenters, Electricians and Seamstresses, and all those other craftsmen and women whose work goes to make up the sum total which is the Theatrical Art, may be encouraged, and taught, so that they can be enabled adequately to hold up to the people from whence they sprung that mirror which can never lie so long as there is a hand to hold it, and a stage to stand upon. The Theatre Company knows its job, but it is sadly handicapped for want of plays which portray Durham people, and their problems, their needs, desires, hopes and aspirations. Such plays can only be written and such theatre can only be used by people who have a strong sense of social responsibility, and purpose. The theatre is a weapon, as well as a mirror. It can bludgeon into stupor, or it can arouse to awareness. It is not a toy for tired, or dilettante younglings, or oldsters to amuse themselves with. The 'Everyman Company' knows that and, even now, in the difficult days of war, knows that its theatre can do its true job better than ever it did before, knows the kind of plays that ought to be written but which are not available as yet. It has just concluded a highly successful run of a Afinoginyev's 'Distant Point', a production which definitely marks an historic moment in its life, but 'Distant Points' are not written every day. Durham will, however, yet find its own dramatists. The 'Everyman Theatre' has some in the making now, and is likely to produce more. It may yet become the 'Abbey' Theatre of Durham County.

Such then are some of the things the Settlement has done and hopes to do, and when the possibilities are latent and its aims and methods are more widely understood it may become clear to the larger people's organisations that they themselves should enter more fully into its work and, from that co-operation, it may become the People's University of Durham, financed and controlled by the people and for the people, a college where the Mining Sciences take pride of place, from where the Social Sciences, Politics, Economics and Trade Union Organisations will be studied side by side with the study and practice of the creative arts, in a theatre of its own, for they also are all Social Sciences, and are indivisible. One without the other is but a key without a lock. The Settlement will then indeed have fulfilled most of its main functions and, as such, it can either pass out, or pass on to some other place at the command of the Social Science School to begin its work all over again. The Settlement has worked towards that and for eleven years, it is just that eleven years nearer to it, and there are some signs now of a much wider understanding, for that vision, which it has seen so clearly, can now be seen by others, and by the time this War ends there will be such a demand, and need for creative activities, that that vision may materialise even in the life-time of our own very much mauled generations who have known nothing but destructive wars, of one kind or another, for many years.

The Spennymoor Settlement then believes in, and works for firstly, economic security for all, and secondly, for freedom and ample facilities for every man, woman and child to develop their individual facilities and gifts without fear of sectional exploitation, but for the wealth and happiness of all. That way is long and hard to travel, but some of the road is charted. One map has been made, and is issued most hopefully here and now, in the dark days of the last World War. It is issued by the Spennymoor Settlement and is headed, 'The Durham People's University'. Sections of the road are shown marked as 'Durham School of Mining Technology', 'Durham

School of Social Science', 'Durham Nursery School's Association', and 'Durham People's Theatre'. These last two may seem strangely out of place but the road must be traversed if the goal is to be reached, and held. Who will walk that road, comrades on a great adventure? The Spennymoor Settlement hopes and expects to be there. What other of the people's organisations will assist and will accompany it? Will the great Trades Unions be there?

The last war was followed by an outcrop of Memorials in most of our towns and villages. Is it too fantastic to suggest that this War and its sacrifices for the freedom of the peoples should be commemorated by beginning even now, in a small way, with the foundation and erection of an institution such as is all too briefly indicated here? Or is it wicked, even to suggest, let alone propose, that such a vast, and obviously dynamic kind of monument should be raised in proof that a great good can indeed arise out of great evil?

Bill Farrell 1942

Appendix 3: Curtain Calls

Distant Point by Alexander Afinogenov, January 26th – 31st 1942

Cast list:- George Roantree, John Bray, Peggy Claughan, Victor Hardaker, Alf Bates, Norman Cornish, John Murray, W.G. Farrell, E. Ceridwen Farrell, Carrie Johnson and Iris Bray

The Spennymoor Settlement

They Came to a City by J. B. Priestley, March 21st – 24th and June 11th – 16th 1945

Original set design by Mitchell McKenzie

Cast list:- E. Ceridwen Farrell, Mary Coverdale, George Roantree, Ivy Gillans, W.G. Farrell, Edith Harris, Geoffrey Cates, Patricia French and John Murray.

The Mother by Maxim Gorky, November 11th - 13th 1948

Cast list:- Jean Grainger, A.E. Spence, E. Ceridwen Farrell, Reginald Martin, Robert Welch, Ivy Bennett, James B. Storey, W.G. Farrell, Iris Bray, Betty Wendel and Anne Wendel.

The Corn is Green by Emlyn Williams, December 11th – 13th 1952

Cast list:- Wilfred Jolly, Muriel Lamb, John Smith, Mavis Blair, Chris Alker, Fred Dunn, Sylvia Owen, Carrie Johnson, E. Ceridwen Farrell, W. Gillespie, Robert Bee, Victor Lamb, Robert Welch, W.G. Farrell and Margaret Thompson.

Robert's Wife by St. John Ervine, October 18th – 22nd 1955

Cast list:- Hazel Wendel, Brenda Cummins, Molly Gash, Edith Kirtley, Bill Soulsby, Fred Lightfoot, Robert Welch, Cicely Milburn, James B. Storey, Trevor Airey, Jack Webb, Betty Wendel and Wilfred Jolly.

The Spennymoor Settlement

The Same Sky by Yvonne Mitchell, October 2nd – 4th 1958

Cast list:- Brenda Cummins, Peter Robson, Neil Moult, Muriel Lamb, Robert Welch, Muriel Kelly, Hazel Welch, James Mason, James B. Storey, George Bushell and Molly Gash.

One of Those Days by Kent Richards, June 14th – 16th 1962

Cast list:- Doreen Ferguson, Maude Sinclair, Edith Kirtley, Carrie Johnson, Colin M. Kennedy, Brenda Savage, Malcolm Marsden, James B. Storey and Muriel Lamb.

The Spennymoor Settlement

Serious Charge by Philip King, November 14th – 16th 1963

Cast list:- Edith Kirtley, Betty Chisholm, Vivien Campbell, Jack Kane, Frank Saunders, June Boden, and James Mason.

The Late Edwina Black by William Dinner and William Morum, June 18th – 20th 1970

Cast list:-, Frances Morgan, Edith Kirtley, George Rowntree and George Brydon.

The Last Act by Myra Williams, December 7th – 9th 1989

Cast list:-, Elsie E. Hands, Lilian E. Whitehead, Marilyn Imerson, Edith Kirtley, Marion Jackson and Eileen Mason.

Beautiful Forever by Glyn Jones, May 6th – 8th 1993

Cast list:- Elsie Hands, Edith Kirtley, Jaimie Archer, Carolyn McAdam, Marion Jackson and Lilian Whitehead.

The Spennymoor Settlement

Blithe Spirit by Noel Coward, May 18th – 20th 1995

Cast list:- Sharon Crosby, Elsie Hands, Michael Hampel, James B. Storey, Sylvia Dobson, Lilian Whitehead and Marion Jackson.

bibliography

Abley, Bob, Spennymoor Remembered Book 2. ARB Publications. 2000

Armstrong, Keith, Homespun. Northern Voices. nd

Beavis, Dick, What Price Happiness?

Beveridge, William, Power and Influence. Hodder & Stoughton 1953

Briggs, A. and A. Macartney, Toynbee Hall: first hundred years. Routledge and Keagan Paul, 1984.

Chaplin, S., Smell of Sunday Dinner. Frank Graham 1971

Cornish, N., A Slice of Life. Mallabar. 1979

Farrell, W.G., Diaries 1940 – 1954

Farrell, W.G., Spennymoor Settlement Archive. University Library, Palace Green, Durham City

Farrell, W.G., Way to the Better 1942

Freeman, M., History of Education 2002. Volume 31 p245 – 262 'No finer school than a settllement.'

Harrison, J.F.C., Learning and Living 1790 – 1960. Routledge and Keagan Paul. 1961

Johnson, C., Strength in Community: An introduction to the history and impact of the Settlement Movement. BASSAC 2000

McManners, R. and G. Wales, Shafts of Light. Gemini Productions. 2002

McManners, R. and G. Wales, Tom McGuinness: The art of an underground miner. Gemini Productions. 1997

Mansbridge, A., An Adventure in Working Class Education – being the story of the WEA – 1903 – 1915. Longmans. 1920

Mason, William, A Study of One Aspect of Adult Education: The residential settlement. Dissertation. 1954

Newsom, J., Out of the Pit. Blackwell. 1936

Pimlott, J.A.R., Toynbee Hall: 50 years of social progress 1884 – 1934. Dent 1935

Robertson, W., Where Hope Lives. Headline. 2001

Spennymoor Settlement 21st Birthday Commemorative Magazine. 1951

Vicinus, M., Independent Women: work and community for single women 1850 – 1923. Virago. 1985